Constructing
Your Dissertation

*A Guide for Students as They Begin Their
Doctoral Research.*

Jess L. Gregory, Ed.D.

.

Edition 1.1

ISBN: 1537351613
ISBN-13: 978-1537351612

Preface

In working with students as they develop their research, it became clear to me that it would help to have some guidelines that might act like a portable pocket-sized coach or advisor. There are a multitude of scholarly, comprehensive books that examine every detail of the dissertation process. This monograph does not aspire to that. Rather, it is designed to be a small stepping-stone.

Each section that follows is intended to be a gentle introduction so that a student can then judge what level of support they need for that particular part of their process. I asked my students to ask me questions so that this monograph is guided by student needs rather than by what I think a student wants. Hopefully, it will answer some of the questions that a student may not even know that he or she needs to ask as he/she begins the process of developing pertinent research. A critical part of the research process is asking good questions in a timely manner. The challenge in this is that while the question may be new to the researcher, it is likely not new to the person to whom the question is posed. Choosing which questions to ask and which to investigate independently is an art.

This text will likely answer some of the more basic questions, freeing the reader to ask the questions that will spark intellectual conversations with his or her dissertation committee, ultimately producing a stronger dissertation document. The dissertation writing process is a once-in-a-

lifetime experience to be celebrated, a process in which --
authors can be fully immersed in their own research and have
the support of a team of experts to support their endeavor.
Seek to appreciate the experience and have the deep
conversations with your team, to not only build your argument,
but also, to carve a place in academia for yourself!

Table of Contents

Acknowledgements

I owe a debt of gratitude to my current and former students at Southern Connecticut State University and at the University of Bridgeport. Working alongside them as they define and conduct their research has given me the experience required to create this monograph. It is my sincere hope that the shared learning in the dissertation process was as valuable to them as it was to me. I would also like to thank my former professors, especially the ones that held high standards and kept me accountable, even when I would have preferred to offer excuses. Among that group are Drs. Roberta Stewart (Dartmouth), Jeremy Rutter (Dartmouth), and Vincent Breslin (SCSU), thank you.

I would also like to acknowledge the generous and caring practitioners who wrote letters of advice included in this volume. Finally, I would like to recognize my colleagues. I see what they offer students, and this has enhanced my own capability. I am fortunate to work with such gifted professionals.

Sample Table of Contents for a Proposal

This table is not double-spaced for the purposes of saving paper; in your document, it would be-double spaced if you are required to follow APA 6th edition. Remember that your program's guidelines supersede APA formatting if there is ever a difference between the two. Niralee K. Patel-Lye has granted permission to use her table of contents.

1

Sample Table of Contents for a Full Dissertation

This table is not double-spaced for the purposes of saving paper; in your document, it would be double-spaced if you are required to follow APA 6th edition. Niralee K. Patel-Lye has granted permission to use her table of contents.

TABLE OF CONTENTS

Chapter 1: Introduction

The following details are based on the varied experiences of my students and should be seen as a collection of opinions. There are a multitude of comprehensive texts available on preparing your dissertation; this is merely a guide as you begin your journey.

That disclaimer aside, I intend to use an overarching analogy throughout this work, not because it is the only analogy that will work (indeed, many will) but because you are embarking on a single large project that can be broken down into a series of steps, like the building of a new home. Each part of your dissertation will be explained through the lens of this analogy. Ultimately, the work you put into your degree creates equity based on the choices you make and the quality of the structure and finish, just like the equity that is amassed when you construct a home.

A Little Overview of Each Chapter of a Traditional Dissertation

A traditional dissertation format includes five chapters which work together to establish your academic credentials and serve as your admission ticket into the academy. Other formats for dissertations or different capstone experiences can serve the same purpose, but for this guide, the focus will remain fixed on the five-chapter format. Discuss with your program what options you have available, as far as the format for your product; perhaps the traditional format is best for you, but be sure to make an informed choice.

The introduction or first chapter "hooks" the reader. You must establish an undeniable need to study this topic and demonstrate that you understand how everything fits together in the big picture. Your introduction can generate the energy that compels the reader to continue reading, to see how you intend to answer the research questions and discover what you will ultimately find. Even so, chapter one is a bit of a tease; you draw in the reader without sharing every detail of the study and without letting the reader know what you found. You mention how you bound your study (limitations and delimitations) but only briefly, just enough to establish a need for the reader to keep going. You tell the reader what you mean with definitions and provide a structure and organization that will keep the reader on the path you have chosen for them to follow.

Some of this path is determined by how you organize your review of the literature, which happens in chapter two. While a reader expects you to comprehensively address the relevant scholarship available, how you present that information remains at your discretion. You create an argument based on the published works of those that have come before you. Remember, they may have more experience now, but they were once doctoral students too! If one of the key players in your area of research is local, reach out to them. Who knows? if you invite him/her for a cup of coffee or tea, that key player just might say yes!

Chapter two also demonstrates that you are well-read and knowledgeable. A high-quality chapter two includes the seminal work connected to a topic and the newest published scholarship into a well-crafted argument. What are the big ideas around your topic? Who is talking about them? What are they saying? Do they all agree? How does this fit with the surrounding relevant issues? Have you addressed every variable in your study? [A note here: rhetorical devices, like rhetorical questions, have no place in formal academic writing.

Good for me this is not a formal piece of academic writing! If it were, I would have to find a way to get to the essence of the questions and actually craft a well-written paragraph which includes transitions between ideas.] A final note on the expectations of chapter two: it is imperative that you address your degree in chapter two. If you are seeking to earn a degree in leadership, then you will want to make sure you include the relevant literature that addresses a leadership issue you have identified. Some students find it difficult to connect their passion to the actual title of the degree they are seeking; please note you should not skimp here. Indulge yourself in some soul searching, if required, to make the connection clear to yourself before you start trying to write or even outline chapter two. The time you spend thinking this through now will garner a high investment return in your final dissertation product.

Thinking in advance is critical for chapter three as well. An ill-conceived chapter three can derail a student's progress toward a degree. During coursework, professors talk about methods, whether they are mixed, quantitative or qualitative, but the methodology includes not just how you will answer your research questions, but also partially defines you as a researcher. The choices you make in chapter three speak volumes about your values and your goals. Do spend some time finding research articles or dissertations that you respect, even if they are in a different discipline, and seek to discover what elements you are connecting with. Reflect on why you feel those connections. Your committee will offer some input into your methodological approach; it is important to remember that the advice you receive is a reflection of their values and goals as a researcher. Ultimately, though, *you* are conducting this research, so the plan you create has to work for you. A well-formed draft of the first three chapters is generally presented in some fashion, such as a proposal, so that you can solicit feedback from a greater audience before you actually begin conducting the research.

Before you can conduct your research project, you need to secure IRB approval; then, it is time to put chapter three into action, generating the results that will be reported in chapter four. Frequently, chapters four and five are written in tandem. As you generate the results and outputs of your study, organizing them by research question, you are likely thinking about what they may mean. Keep track of those thoughts comprise chapter five. Sadly, this type of reflection does not belong in chapter four. This makes chapter four difficult to write, relative to transitions and flow. Fortunately, many scholars have already written dissertations; pull a few from programs you respect in which the author used a similar method to collect his or her data and follow these models. Your research is new; you do not have to recreate the dissertation format.

Finally, with chapter four presenting your results, you are ready to write chapter five with your conclusions. I can tell you from experience that despite my dissertation chair/sponsor telling me that it would, chapter five did not write itself. I failed to keep track of my ideas when I was writing chapter four, which resulted in my slogging through chapter five. I found it difficult to pull together all the ideas I had generated when I was analyzing my data with the relevant literature in chapter two, and address the problem I had established in chapter one. Reflecting on this, working on an outline of chapter five while I was writing chapter four would have resulted in an easier time. I now suggest writers go back into the outlines they created for chapters one and two to make sure that the ideas that were important enough to be included in the first two chapters are addressed in chapter five, and that chapter five includes very clear answers to the research questions. Let's be honest; you have to actually answer the question that you said was so important to study!

So, briefly, those are the five chapters. Later in this text each chapter will be explored in greater detail, and for each chapter, I will offer you a self-assessment that will help you determine whether your draft is ready to show your dissertation committee. In the next chapters I will offer advice on how to navigate the shift from coursework to working on an independent project, and how you can structure your committee to maximize your experience. Once the human side of the dissertation process has been examined, I will delve into each chapter more fully, capitalizing on my home-building analogy.

Chapter 2: From Coursework to Independence

When you decided to pursue your doctorate, you knew at some point, you would be working independently. Knowing that this will happen and experiencing it are two very different things. Course after course, someone else has been providing the syllabus, the timeline, the evaluation of whether you are making sufficient progress; now, it is up to you. Liberating, exciting, and daunting are all words that can be used to describe the initial energy that cohabits with this newfound independence.

This parallels the emotions I experienced when I had my first apartment in N.Y.C. with no roommates, parents, or anyone else to whom I must answer. I needed to be vigilant about minding my keys so I didn't lock myself out, but I could keep my place as neat or as messy as I wanted. I could redecorate on a whim. I was the only person I had to answer to. It was great-until I got a cold. There was no one to go to the store for me, or make me soup, or offering to bring me a cup of tea. I could get food delivered, but that required me to get out of bed to answer the door. I was the only person I could lean on...except my friends.

During your coursework, you were with other doctoral students who are now working independently as well. I am here to tell you that while your work is independent, you don't have to go it alone. One way to excel during this self-regulated phase of your degree is to develop an accountability group. You may have one or more people in your program with whom you have connected; don't lose touch. Keep a regular meeting time, and report to each other how things are going.

An accountability partner or group helps you monitor your progress. Each week, meet and briefly report what you have accomplished since last the time you were together. After a little personal reconnection time, and maybe even some food and drink, a period lasting roughly thirty minutes, each person reports for two to three minutes on what they have accomplished, and the one next step they plan to do. The group listens and offers constructive suggestions on how to support or help the person in that next step. Once everyone has reported out, about one hour into the meeting, then everyone works for twenty minutes, breaks for five, and repeats the process for two more rounds. This pattern, called the pomodoro technique[1], builds a maintainable work pace, respecting the brain's need for breaks. In all, this meeting takes about 2-2.5 hours, roughly the time that you used to spend in one class.

If you present this meeting time to yourself and your loved ones as required time each week, just like the classes you used to attend, it eases the transition to the dissertation phase. Some students find that they start strong and then get lost during the process of writing their proposal. Perhaps they have accepted a promotion that demands more time and attention than their prior position, or changes in their personal life that distract them from working on their proposal. Ultimately, there are many things that can get in the way of the timely completion of a dissertation proposal or completed manuscript. Planning to protect your time and attention at the outset can increase the likelihood that you will achieve success.

To be fair, not everything that will demand your time is within your control. I have had doctoral students who couldn't

---

[1] More information on this technique can be found at
http://pomodorotechnique.com/.

get their family on board as far as carving out quiet time, and they found themselves packing their research into a suitcase and checking into a quiet hotel to get their writing done. Other students have relegated themselves to the basement, where they can spread out their work without it being disturbed. Still others found they had no problem working on it while their kids were doing homework. Whether it is traveling to campus and using a room in the library or student center, going to the public library, or sitting at your kitchen table, find a time and space that works for you and build a habit around moving your dissertation forward.

Another helpful strategy exists in the digital space. Perhaps setting aside a dedicated space in your home is not possible, and maybe meeting weekly on campus like you did during your coursework phase is also untenable. All is not lost; you can use an online space in place of an in-person accountability group. A myriad of online tools[2] take group emails and texts to the next level. While a gentle reminder, set in your calendar, might be enough to protect your working time, I have found that being accountable to others works better that being accountable to myself alone.

Committing a whole day to working may generate energy around your dissertation when you start to feel stuck. You can frame it as a work party, or bootcamp; it doesn't really matter what you call it, as long as work gets done. Not everyone can take a whole day to move their project forward, but if you can, really protect the time. The laundry will wait. For me, a non-basketball fan, March Madness is a great time to

---

[2] At the time of this writing, Google hangouts are popular, https://hangouts.google.com/ but there are many free and paid tools that will allow multiple presenters (gotomeeting, https://www.gotomeeting.com; WebEx, https://signup.webex.com) and apps such as BlueJeans (https://bluejeans.com/) that will permit you to meet in a virtual space.

get work done without feeling like I am abandoning my spouse. He gets to watch all the games he wants and I get lots of writing time, so it's a win, win! Sure, March Madness comes but once a year, but many other diversionary pursuits can free up work time without guilt. You get to be a little selfish. While the rest of the family attends a picnic or birthday party, you might stay back and work. Consider sending your family to see a movie! You will, if you are creative, find lots of "found time" to work.

That being said, you also need to take breaks and reward yourself. I gave myself a little gift for the completed draft of each chapter. Nothing too extravagant; just a little extra to celebrate the milestone. Reflecting back, each of those gifts is collecting dust now (the Wii Fit and Atari 2600 come to mind) but at the time, I used them happily. Each time I played a game of Pac-Man™ on the Atari, I was celebrating the completion of my draft of chapter three being deemed "really close" by my committee. I didn't want to reward myself with food, as it was tough enough making time to exercise. Consider ways you can reward yourself as you move forward.

Not always smooth

The process of writing a dissertation ebbs and flows, with great days when everything seems to fit together and make sense, and other days when nothing flows and doubt reigns supreme. If you don't have an accountability partner or group and your family isn't 100% on board, it can be a very lonely process. Still, even if you are going it alone, there are things you can do to support yourself on the rough days.

One strategy includes keeping an idea journal or notebook. Make sure to pick something that you can keep with you, digital or paper; any time you have an idea connected to your dissertation, write it down! This journal serves as an external memory of connections for when you are having a hard day and don't see how any of this fit together. You can reread your ideas and see how you thought it might work.

18

Voice to text features on tablets and smart phones are great for recording ideas as they happen. I just have to mention this: DO NOT WRITE/TEXT WHILE YOU ARE DRIVING. Call your house or office and leave yourself a voicemail that you can later write down. The idea may be wonderful, but if you have an accident because you were driving while distracted, it wont really matter how brilliant it was.

A cousin of the idea journal, mind-mapping or concept-mapping, can aid you in making explicit connections between ideas. Frequently your gut may lead you to connect ideas, and while you trust your gut, it is hard to explain why the ideas connect. Creating a map of the ideas forces you to write down all the possible connections[3]. As you write, the map aids in the organization of ideas and in developing the transitions between ideas. A map also helps you delimit your study, choosing what to include and what to exclude to focus narrowly on your research questions. Without a map, it is difficult to maintain a focus, but more about that in chapter 4.

Speaking of focus, developing productive procrastination strategies is very helpful. I am sure the kitchen could stand to be be cleaned, but that will not move you toward your goal of completing your degree. By the way, my house was never cleaner than when I was working on my dissertation, so while I am saying this to you, I was unable to consistently take my own advice. There are some tasks that are tedious, require little thinking, but are very important to your ultimate success. Checking the format of tables, charts and references are all productive procrastination strategies. Another such venture is creating your list of tables and figures. Setting your styles if you are using MS Word to match the required dissertation format and then applying the styles to headings and

---

[3] This chapter walks through how to use a concept map to define variables: Gregory, J. L. (2012). Concept mapping, finding your way. In B. P. Skott & M. Ward (Eds.), *Active Learning Exercises for Research Methods in Social Sciences*. Thousand Oaks, CA: Sage.

subheadings will save time at the end when you are generating a table of contents. Another procrastination strategy includes checking your references to ensure that you have a 1:1 alignment. Through all the versions, edits, and drafts reference lists tend to get messy. Use some down time to clean your list.

I have found that reading about writing is a less productive but pleasantly indulgent form of procrastination. I know, you are reading about writing your dissertation now, but everything in moderation. Many well-intentioned authors have written texts to help you, and some are quite good, but remain aware that any time you spend reading about writing is time you are not spending actually writing. If you indulge in this procrastination, set a reasonable boundary; a chapter, a book, a time limit, something that will remind you that it is time to get back to the work at hand.

I am not sure whether I have really faced this, but there are lots of authors with suggestions as to how to deals with writer's block. Don't get me wrong, there are times when I can't form a useful sentence, but I never considered it writer's block. Perhaps this is because I don't think of myself as a writer. Nevertheless, if you find that you are stuck, you can look back at your idea journal, review your map or indulge in some productive procrastination to unstick yourself. One strategy to combat writer's block is stopping mid-sentence.

> Always stop when you are going good and don't think about it or worry about it until you start to write the next day. That way your subconscious will work on it all the time. But if you think about it consciously or worry about it you will kill it and your brain will be tired before you start. This way you can get back into your writing flow with greater ease (Hemingway, Seldes, Dreiser, Hughes, & Ficke, 1935).

Finally, sometimes you have to walk away. Literally. When nothing is going right with your writing, stop! Go for a walk, but bring your phone in case the walk frees up an idea you need to record. Some of my best sentences have been narrated to my phone to type. Then, I get home and can write again. One time I was really stuck at the start of chapter five of my dissertation. I called my cousin Leah, cried a bit, and implored her for advice. She asked me when the last time I saw a movie was. I told her I had not gone to see a movie since I started working on my dissertation. She suggested I do just that. After watching some bit of Hollywood fluff I was able to get back to work. You may find yourself at a place where you have to do something very different, become totally disengaged for a little while; respect that you may actually need that, and then get back to work.

Mind your expectations

This section focuses mainly on how to manage your expectations so that your level of frustration is reduced. One of my current doctoral student recites the mantra, "Cap not cape!" Surely the work you do will be important, and may influence policy and practice, but it is not your life's work. You are more than one document. You are not saving the whole of education with your dissertation. When it starts to feel overwhelming, remember the goal is completing your dissertation and earning your degree.

One way to increase your anxiety and displeasure with the dissertation process is to constantly compare your pace with that of a colleague. Every dissertation evolves at it's own pace. How you choose to access data to answer your research question, the composition of your committee and even the research question itself all play a role in the pace towards your degree. This is a once-in-a-lifetime experience, and, while you don't want to languish in an all but dissertation (ABD) state, you also don't want to rush the experience.

I wish someone had told me not to rush when I was working toward my degree. I relentlessly pushed myself, binge writing for days on end. It was the summer after my comprehensive exams and I did very little other than work on my dissertation. I took no time to reflect on the process or my personal and emotional health. One of my dissertation committee members and now a friend and colleague, Lori Noto, called me her stalker. She provided me great feedback, but it took a while to get it from her. In hindsight, she returned my work within two weeks, sometimes even within a single week, which was more than timely! I hounded her for the feedback, sometimes twice a week. She had every reason to set me straight, but chose not to—she just ignored my pestering, and when the feedback was ready, she gave it to me.

As soon as my committee provided me feedback, I rushed to implement every word. I did not consider the implications of these suggested changes, I just made them. I am not going to suggest that you read my dissertation as an example of high quality work; if you find it, just know I have learned a lot since then. Part of writing a dissertation is becoming an expert in one very small area: the area you define for your research. When you receive feedback, consider the feedback before blindly implementing it. You are the nascent expert, your committee provides you feedback, and will evaluate the ultimate quality of your product, but nobody will be more of an expert in your topic that you. Maintain a pace of work that allows you to become that expert.

OK, one more example. It isn't just me that is impatient. I received this email from one of my doctoral students, sent Monday 10-17 at 3:49pm:

> I'm a little concerned because I haven't received any feedback. I'm starting to panic a little bit because I'm not sure if I haven't received feedback because there's something really wrong with the proposal or because they haven't received the appendices. I delivered the hard copy. I dropped them off but had to leave them by their office doors (by the time I got to campus on Friday, it was almost 10 pm).

I can smile about this one, because I was this person's mentor. I explained to them that her committee was not expected to

22

come to campus on the weekend. When she and I discussed it, it was worthy of a chuckle. To her it seemed like an eternity, but to the rest of the world she had allowed the committee less than a day to review her work.

You don't have to be the expert... yet

Although you are becoming the expert in your field, you aren't fully cooked yet! And, since you have not written a dissertation before, you don't have to know everything there is to know about writing a dissertation. You do want to seek out the resources you will need to be successful, such as the program handbook, the university's guidelines and your style guide (i.e., APA manual). That being said, you know the person in class who asks questions that are answered in the syllabus? You don't want to be that person. If the answer is in the aforementioned resources, then don't ask it! One important exception is when there are apparent contradictions. The APA manual (I am sure other style guides agree) states that the program's guidelines supersede the information provided within the manual (*Publication Manual of the American Psychological Association*, 2009), but some programs and universities develop their guidelines in isolation. What can happen is that one changes something without the other one noticing, when that happens, you the student are likely to notice it first, so ask.

Other great questions to pose come out of your early research. "I was reading so and so and thought... what do you think?" Notice how this question confirms that you have done some initial reading and thinking before asking the question, and how it is open-ended. The ideal response to this question comes in the form of a content-based discussion. These early, big questions are not limited to your committee members. If you know someone who is knowledgeable, ask. There are also discussion boards and other online spaces where these types of questions are asked[4]. Some of these tools, like ReserchGate, allow you to connect with and "follow" researchers. This can be very helpful once you have conducted an initial literature review and know who the key researchers influencing your topic are. You can request full-text articles through the site, sometimes even getting to read research before it has been officially published.

Conclusion

As you move from the structured phase of your doctoral pursuits to the open and exciting part of your degree, you will take an active role in determining your experience. Just like moving out on your own, you will assess whether something meets your expectations, and if it doesn't, what you can do about it. While there are still some supports in place (like when you call a friend to sit with you during your first thunderstorm in a new place—wait, that wasn't you? That was me?) you have the responsibility to make this move to independence a success.

You have what you need to embark on this journey; if you didn't, you wouldn't have gotten this far. Try out different strategies to determine what will be effective for you as you keep working toward your goal of earning your degree. Not everyone likes using the pomodoro technique; for some people, cleaning the kitchen is a necessary pre-writing activity. Find what is effective for you, and every day, you will move closer to graduation.

---

[4] ResearchGate is a free site that is currently being used for this type of purpose (https://www.researchgate.net/). Do take care as this sort of surfing and researching can become a procrastination tool.

Chapter 3: Picking a Strong Committee

Picking your doctoral committee can be anxiety-inducing. This group of scholars will be facilitating (or inhibiting) your progress toward the ultimate goal of earning the doctorate, like your contractors in the house-building analogy.. Since they play such a crucial role, it behooves you, or any other student, to purposefully investigate the possible committee members. A lot of this depends on the type of person you are. A good fit for one doctoral candidate is a misfit for another, so asking one person's opinion may lead you down a bad path.

To determine what type of committee members you are interested in recruiting, you would benefit from some soul-searching and reflection on who you are as a student, and even more relevantly, as a writer. WHAT?! Not everyone is a gifted writer?! Ok, kidding aside, some people need more support in writing than others. If you, like me, intensely dislike writing, then finding a mentor (sponsor/chair/general contractor) who is a positive, motivating force will be important—you want a cheerleader. Some people actually find joy in writing, for those individuals, a mentor that will ensure that the ideas do not get lost in the writing would be more appropriate—a critic.

Benner (2014) wrote a blog that offers a *Cosmopolitan*-style quiz[5] to help you determine what type of

---

[5] The link to the quiz: http://blog.influenceandco.com/quiz-wh at-type-of-writer-are-you-and-how-to-make-it-work-for-your-content

writer you are and where you may struggle. I am not suggesting that this brief quiz will serve as a substitute for reflection, but if you are not a natural soul-searcher, then it may be a good place to get the reflective juices flowing! Consider your goals as far as writing goes; are you looking only to complete the dissertation, or perhaps present or publish along the way? This is part of who you are as a writer and will influence your choice. Also, determine what sort of personal support network you have in place. Do you have a strong cohort who will effectively prop up your motivation if it flags, or do you need a mentor who will be able to do that?

The mentor's role

Whether your program refers to mentors, sponsors, chairs or some other title, this individual will play a large role in your doctoral experience. He/she serves as the point person at the University and acts as your guide through this process. The mentor holds a great deal of influence; ultimately he or she, with the rest of the committee, will determine whether you have earned your doctorate (Lunenburg & Irby, 2008). Your mentor can help you form the rest of your dissertation committee. While each program sets requirements for the composition of a dissertation committee, those merely indicate the requirements. They do not outline how to craft a committee that will best meet your individualized needs.

Your mentor is a huge influence on the direction of your research, so you want to pick someone who is knowledgeable about your intended research area. They do not need to be an expert in your very specific interest (although that would be a best-case scenario), but they need to know the big players and be able to coach you if you get stuck. If your mentor is a great person but is unfamiliar with your area of research, he or she cannot push you to excel in creating a name for yourself in the field. It isn't a matter of he or she doesn't want what is best; he/she just won't know enough about the nuances to ask you the challenging questions that will drive you toward the highest quality dissertation.

Your intended mentor's level of expertise will drive the quality of feedback you receive, and steer you towards the most relevant methods to answer your research question(s). Each researcher will have a varying level of comfort with and attitude toward research methodologies. Attitudes towards research methodologies stem from a researcher's paradigm. A research paradigm stems from one's ontology and epistemology (Guba & Lincoln, 1994; Guba, 1990). Here again: *it is important for you to know yourself*[6]. Does your ontology, your view on the nature of reality, align with that of your possible sponsor? How about the way you view the relationship with knowledge and how we uncover or discover that knowledge (epistemology)? These two elements of your researcher stance influence all your research-related decisions. If you and your mentor are misaligned, then you will have to work harder at communicating any of your research ideas. Finally, these factors determine which research methodologies will be most relevant to your research, and the methods you use to evaluate your research question(s). Not every mentor views all research methods and methodologies the same; be sure to determine if your potential mentor will support methods that are consistent with your paradigm.

If you pick a mentor (or committee member) that is not meeting your needs, check your program's policies about changing. You will have to be comfortable discussing your needs with your mentor and being transparent about your feelings if your needs are not being met. Sure, switching a mentor may involve some difficult conversations, but you only

---

[6] There are many websites that have more detail on research paradigms, one such site is:
http://www.slideshare.net/eLearnCenter/research-methods-uoc-2013
that includes 56 slides covering the basics.

get to complete your dissertation once, and you deserve a positive experience. Your mentor's role is to steward your progress. There can also be times when your mentor's job is to reign you in. You need to be able to trust your mentor, and know that he or she is interested in supporting your success. Your mentor's experience guides his or her advice to you, and while it must be respected, it was also based on experience with different students. Your situation may be different, *but* you picked the mentor for their experience and advice—this is not the time to be closed to receiving feedback. Seriously weigh the factors that cause you to consider changing a mentor before you act. Changing mentors may be the right move, but you want to weigh the costs and benefits; make sure that the delay it will cause is worth it.

Other Considerations

Ideally, your mentor will serve as your bridge into academia, providing informal mentoring and networking support long after you have earned your degree. The nature of that future relationship depends on the quality of the experience that you have when you are working on your degree. In addition to the personality match, also consider the mentor's level of accessibility. Avoid choosing a mentor that has applied for a sabbatical, which could mean they are unavailable for a semester or a year. You may also want to look at the frequency of your mentor's travel schedule. While most mentors will also have a teaching commitment, up to four classes a semester, there may be other demands on the mentor's time such as committee work, consulting jobs, grant work, research and writing deadlines, and other doctoral students. While many mentors balance a lot of these well, be aware of the competing demands on your possible mentor's time before you finalize your selection.

At tenure-granting institutions, holding or earning tenure also plays a role in your selection process. Tenure earning faculty face a high-stakes process, generally in their sixth year at a university, where they could possibly leave the university if they are not granted tenure. During this tenure earning period, faculty feel pressure to produce and may be overcommitted. This is a mixed blessing, as the tenure-earning professor may feel an increased pressure to support your success and support you as you begin to publish. The general rule of thumb is that you retain first authorship of work you create and work resulting from data you collect, but appreciation for committee support shows up in listing committee members that have helped you develop your project as later authors on the paper or presentation, in order of contribution. Do not list anyone as an author that did not contribute to your work.

The contribution toward your success generally exists in the form of feedback on early conceptual brainstorming, and later in comments on drafts. When you think about your possible mentor, do you value his/her input? If you do not value what the mentor has to offer to your research idea, he or she is not the right mentor for you! You need your mentor to give you tough love, accurate appraisals of the quality of your thinking and your writing. If you have not had the mentor candidate as a professor, you may have to ask around to other students that have had the professor in class or as a mentor. You want someone that will read your work thoroughly and provide a thoughtful critique.

Another question to ask when you reach out to other students or alumni centers on the time to completion for most students that this mentor advises. Some faculty push students to complete in a timely manner, while others have a track record of students taking longer to complete. Look at the overall average number of semesters that students have required to complete their degree, but keep in mind that this is only partially controlled by the mentor. Students pursuing their doctorate have competing demands on their time, very few of which can be influenced by a mentor. Some students take on new and time-consuming promotions, have families, or undergo other life events that distract them from focusing on their dissertation.

Forming your committee

On a more positive note, your mentor will be your point person, but you will also have at least two more academics helping to shape your dissertation. Together, you and your mentor will determine the composition of your committee. A strong committee meets your individual needs, and aligns with your topic and your future career goals. While some students look for committee members with a top name in their field, others look for members that have complementary skills to the mentor's. If your mentor meets some needs but not all, then the rest of the committee can fill in gaps.

Work with your mentor to build a list of possible committee members, then meet with the potential candidates. Ask them if they have not only a willingness to serve on your dissertation committee, but also the time to do so. Please keep this in mind, this is *your* committee, but coordinating three or more academics' schedules can be a challenge. Remain mindful of the competing demands on your committee members' time. In addition to serving on your committee, academics must conduct and publish their own research, provide service through committee work, and teach up to four classes a semester. This means that setting meeting times or times for a proposal hearing of defense will be a logistical matter, so don't choose someone that lives or works very far away from your home institution, or is overcommitted in other areas and can not give your work a due amount of attention.

In choosing your committee, you want to aim for a balance of knowledge and skills and cohesion. It would become very frustrating to have feuding committee members. One way to avoid this is to present the names of those you are considering to potential committee candidates. This way a candidate can suggest to you if there are individuals with

30

whom he or she does not work well. Most adults can play well with others, but in the microcosm of university life, politics do, unfortunately, play a role.

Streamlining process

With your mentor, you are the point people for making sure progress toward your degree is moving forward consistently. How you do this will vary based on your personality, work style, and the composition of your committee. At the beginning of the relationship with the committee, ask how each member would prefer to receive products for comment. Some mentors will want to be involved before all your elegant writing is applied to ideas, asking to see an outline or a graphic organizer to ensure that the ideas flow before the language is added. Others will want to be involved only once more polished drafts are available. Regardless of their preferences, respect them!

Another preference to be respected is the format of products turned in for comment. More and more, committee members can provide feedback digitally, but that does not necessarily mean that they prefer to do so. Reading a manuscript on paper is different from reading it electronically, and the reader will see different things, depending on how the document is read. This may mean that for one committee member you are providing printed copies, hole-punched and placed in a binder; for another, you are sending an attachment, and for the third, you are sharing a file in the cloud. You want the highest quality feedback you can get from each committee member, so providing your hard work in the preferred format is one way to endear yourself to the committee and glean more of their attention.

Again, based on the discussions you have at the start of the process, you will better know when to share iterations of your work with the different committee members. That said, providing a cover note with each version can facilitate committee members providing the strongest, most focused feedback possible. Your note will cue the committee member to changes that have been made and areas of concern you may have. Aim for specific questions. "I have included Senge as a point of reference, but I am not sure if I have over-developed that section too much making it a distraction. Have I made it sufficiently clear how his work influenced my study without digressing?" This is the sort of question that assures the committee that you are thoughtful in how you are proceeding, that you are the driver of this process, and not just waiting for them to tell you what to do.

You want to avoid sending "rough drafts" to anyone on your committee. Your friends, loved ones, and colleagues can read those. Every time a committee member reads the same paragraph, they are less likely to note small changes or edits that can improve the work overall. A rough draft can cause a committee member to skim. This creates a communication barrier and frustration in that you have the expectation that the committee member gave a thoughtful read to your work and he or she has commented thoroughly, but the committee member saw a rough draft and felt that he or she would have ample more opportunities to provide detailed feedback as the manuscript was closer to being polished. This situation is particularly perilous for those of us who are not instinctive writers.

If you are not a natural grammarian, find someone you know or can afford who will be available to edit drafts before they get to your committee. This is not about APA style (although that is important!); this is about verb agreement types of things and making sure that people are referred to as "who" instead of "that". Whatever your needs, ensure they are met before it gets to your committee. I know that your committee is there to support you, but they are there as experts in the field, not writing experts! If you find that you might need support in that area and don't already know someone, ask around. Many campuses have writing centers or lists of editors. I had a math teacher at the school in which I worked edit my dissertation. She had a keen eye for the grammatical details I couldn't see in my own writing. This is not about your ego, this is not about needing help, this is about creating the highest quality product possible. Giving your committee only polished versions of your work will promote better critiques which further enhance your work.

Conclusion

You are the driver of this process. You determine your committee; with their help, you set the way your committee interacts, as well as the quality of feedback you receive. The committee helps you build your dissertation, and establishes the direction of your research. If you pick a committee that is known for moving students through without much attention to the quality of the product, then you may have created an academic home that will not stand the test of time. If you skimp in the construction, then a strong wind can damage the structure; perhaps to the point of collapse. If you, and your committee attend to details along the way, shore up vulnerable areas as they appear, then the construction of your work will withstand critique and become a lasting source of pride. Build a committee that will support you in conducting and communicating research of the finest quality, earning your degree, and maximizing your personal potential.

Chapter 4: Your First Chapter, The Introduction- The Plans

If we think of your dissertation as a household on unclaimed land, then the introduction serves as the description of the plot you have chosen, along with the plans for your home. With your introduction you tell the reader, and the rest of the academy, why this is the right time and place to build.. You establish which features of this plot are unique and worthy of investing the time and energy to build here. What makes this area special? Who has also built in the area? You create a compelling brochure with a map in chapter one so that others are interested in visiting and know what to look for while they visit.

To create this promotional brochure for your chosen plot, conduct a broad survey of everything that could possibly be relevant. A concept map could be useful here, to help keep track of all the possible topics that relate and their connections (Gregory, 2012). Conducting a comprehensive survey of related topics does a couple of things for you: 1. It helps you frame and situate your chosen research well in the larger landscape and 2. It protects you from questions about why you chose your topic. By cultivating an awareness of all the related areas, you have effectively insulated yourself through preparation. If a colleague, professor, or other academic asks, "why this topic?" you will be well-prepared to provide an elegant reply that is grounded in research.

The introduction of your study will orient the reader. It aims to quickly draw in the reader through establishing the main ideas and context of the study. In the introduction, you communicate what the landscape looks like, painting a picture of the surrounding area and determining which way you will orient your house to take advantage of the best views.

A well-written document is hard to put down. There is a natural flow and economy of words. Each sentence has a purpose -- there is no way to pull out a sentence and have the document still work. When writing a dissertation, it is tempting to add in superfluous sentences to lengthen the document. Resist that temptation! No award exists for the longest dissertation, focus on clarity and economy. To draw the reader in, keep the pace moving with strong transition phrases and sentences.

Transitional words and phrases allow the reader to move from point to point in your document. They boost the understandability and help to clarify the logic in the organization of an argument through illustrating relationships between ideas. Some ideas for transitional words or phrases include:

> as well as, besides, coupled with, furthermore, in addition, likewise, moreover, similarly, accordingly, as a result, consequently, conversely, instead, likewise, on one hand, on the other hand, on the contrary, rather, similarly, yet, but, however, still, nevertheless, in contrast, chiefly, especially, for instance, in particular, markedly, namely, particularly, including, specifically, generally, comparatively, coupled with, correspondingly, identically, likewise, similar, moreover, together with, in essence, in other words, and finally, namely.

Another trick for a transition sentence is to make sure the summative idea for the current paragraph and the paragraph that precedes or follows it are both included in the one sentence. This sentence will serve to connect the thoughts and keep the reader going onto the next idea.

Now that you have the reader following you, with your graceful transitions, ensure they understand fully what you are saying. Many students endeavor to enhance the import of their ideas through obfuscating verbiage. As the last sentence illustrates, the SAT words do not help the reader understand your argument. Just because MS Word lets you right click on a word to get a list of synonyms doesn't mean you should. While this is not the case globally, it is the responsibility of the academic writer in the United States to make points easily understood.

Correspondingly, the organization of the introduction, in conjunction with the writing style, serves to orient the reader in the study. Imagine that this is your site plan. You need this plan to tell the contractors how and where to build your home. It needs sufficient detail to communicate on its own, but not so much that it distracts the reader. This section includes a clear statement of the problem, tight research questions, explains the motivation or rationale for conducting the research and through a detailed description of the context in which the question arises, provides a roadmap for readers. The purpose, problem statement and research questions serve as the backbone for the entire study. Great care should be taken to make sure that the problem, purpose, and research questions are tightly defined and flow naturally from each other.

Statement of the Problem

A problem statement is a clear, concise description of the issue needing to be addressed. It is the focus, the driving force of the study. The heart of a problem statement is just one sentence that describes the problem using very specific language. This is framed in the context of the study with several paragraphs of elaboration. "A problem might be defined as the issue that exists in the literature, theory, or practice that leads to a need for the study" (Creswell, 1994, p.

50). While it may seem like simply stating the problem is like stating the obvious, a very clear problem statement will keep the research focused and balanced.

The statement of the problem is the blueprint for your house. You want it to describe what you are investigating so that the reader knows what you are building. The plan for a ranch looks different from the plans for a colonial; both serve a purpose, but the contractors need to know which they are building. The blueprint shows both how the house will be oriented on the plot of land and what type of home you are building.

The University of Virginia offers one possible brainstorming method with guiding questions to help shape a statement of the problem (Virginia, n.d.; Appendix A). Take your answers to the four questions and put them into fairy-tale order (Status Quo, Destabilizing Moment, Consequences, Resolution). Then, blend those answers into a form that will serve as a problem statement. The problem statement will drive the rest of your study, so it is worth the time to make sure it is saying exactly what you want.

There are other methods for developing a problem statement; all aim toward clarifying the need for your study. If you have not established the "so what" question, then you want to rework this section. The reader needs to come away with a feeling that your research is needed, and that it is a wonder that nobody has sought to address this already. The clarity of your problem statement leads to the impact of your purpose statement.

Purpose of the Study

"The purpose statement should provide a specific and accurate synopsis of the overall purpose of the study" (Locke, Spirduso, & Silverman, 1987, p. 5). Take the time to reflect on what you really want to do with this research. You are not in a rush; time spent at this stage, considering all the possible avenues for your research, will streamline your work further down the line. Here again, clarity in writing and concept are key; if the purpose is not clear to the writer, it cannot be clear to the reader. You want to determine what your home will look like, what types of doors, windows you will have? How will this be your home, distinguishable from other homes? How are you addressing the problem you established in the prior section?

As a part of this synopsis, briefly define and delimit (narrow the scope) of your area of research. It is not essential for you to hit every detail here, as you will be addressing the delimitations more fully in a separate section. Additionally, the purpose of the study foreshadows the questions that will be raised and the hypotheses that will be tested. Again, like the delimitations, these will be addressed more fully later; here, you are merely whetting the reader's appetite.

In addition to piquing interest, this section will clarify your own purpose, as well as directly and explicitly inform the reader. A key feature of the purpose of the study section is a sentence that starts with "The purpose of this study is/was..." Through this section, you will identify the specific method that will be used to investigate the problem, as well as what you will be measuring to evaluate the research questions.

The purpose of the study may include a rationale for the study, or the rationale may be a separate section. The rationale serves to define why the research you are conducting is worthwhile. Firmly and clearly, answer the "so what?" question in a few statements. You started to make the case for the "so what" in the prior section; here you distill that down to its very essence. This section explains the contribution to the general knowledge base, and to the field, that your work presents.

Conceptual Framework

The conceptual framework defines how you are looking at the problem. This is where you align yourself with a tradition. For our home, we may draw on a Craftsman aesthetic, or seek to use more traditional elements. In this section you explain what theory(ies) you believe are involved in your research topic. Your theoretical framework details how the various theories interrelate and draw a conclusion about how the theories connect specifically to your problem.

The conceptual framework will help you justify the methods that you have chosen to investigate your problem. This is where you describe a model of what you think is going on in the problem. If possible, a diagram, figure, or schematic can help model how concepts and theories fit together. You aim to make your own theoretical assumptions and allegiances as explicit as possible; assumptions about other parts of your study and a deeper discussion of theoretical assumptions will be addressed in a later section.

Background

The background section of the dissertation assumes that the reader is unfamiliar with any of the concepts or ideas that are integral to the research. In writing this section, as in the rest of the document, assertions must be supported by references. Keep in mind that this section does not need to contain everything there is to know about the relevant topics, but what the reader needs to know about the topics to understand the arguments you will make in the rest of the document. Here again, that concept map helps you stay focused on what is relevant and delimit out the interesting but non-essential topics.

In providing the reader with the salient information, enough detail must be presented so that they understand the material sufficiently to draw the same empirical, conceptual, and theoretical conclusions. While it is tempting to use this

40

section to provide a more general overview, it is key that the structure directs the reader to the relevant details, the pieces that illustrate the need for (and the importance of) your research.

That is a lot to ask of a single section. This section works in concert with the rest of your dissertation, but it needs to stand on it's own, presenting a fresh, insightful approach to the concepts and details. Try to find a balance between the larger concepts and details so that the reader can see the depth or your understanding. This requires that you critique the research, and organize it *your* way. You are crafting your argument. Take care that this section does not just become a summary or overview of the work of others, and that it contains explicit links between the theory and evidence. One way to think of this section is that it serves as the observed picture of your theoretical framework.

One last word on this section is to be judicious. Choosing the most relevant and respected sources for this section is important. It demonstrates that you know the research, the field, and can identify the seminal works in the field, as well as the important new revelations in your field. More is not always more. An overabundance of sources, or indiscriminant use of references, serve to undermine the reader's confidence in your ability to discern the most relevant research.

In keeping with our home construction metaphor, you don't tell your sub-contractor pouring the foundation of your home what color you intend to paint the walls, but you most assuredly tell him/her where the doors are located and how much weight the foundation will support. In the background you include only the relevant information, arranged in such a way that it provides a full and accurate picture of what is to come.

Research Questions

Directly stemming from the purpose and problem statement of your study are the research questions. The research questions define your research. They are the distillation of what you believe is worthy of study. The importance of the research questions is second only to that of the statement of the problem. Your research questions will directly impact the rest of your dissertation; they will help determine the theoretical framework, the components of the literature review, and the method used to analyze the research questions. If your research questions are unclear, the rest of the dissertation will likely follow suit.

To develop clear research questions, take time to reflect and crystallize your interest in your topic. When you think you are close to your research questions, take a little time to read about what others have written on your topic (or closely related topics). If there is nothing written on your exact topic, then you are filling a gap in the existing literature. It is likely that there are similar studies, but that your population is unique; look at how the other studies were conducted. This step will help you identify a possible method for your research.

In the words of John, Paul, George and Ringo, there's "Nothing you can know that isn't known. Nothing you can see that isn't shown" (Lennon & McCartney, 1967). You are going up against conventional wisdom, looking for a question that has not already been asked and answered. Look at what has been done and pick and choose the best elements to make them your own. Like browsing architectural and home style magazines for inspiration as you develop your building plans, cull the best ideas from many sources to create the ultimate product.

At this point you are close. Begin to bounce the developing questions against trusted sounding boards. You are trying to refine these questions to the point at which they are strong enough to support the whole dissertation project. Your research questions, to be fresh and innovative, must propose a new approach or a novel idea. They should take what has already been done to a new level or to a new population. Once you are confident that the questions are strong, this is the key point where you involve your committee.

But how will you know that your research questions are strong enough? A research question is strong when it is concise, clear, and easily understood. The reader should not wonder exactly what you are studying; it should not be open to debate or subject to interpretation. To facilitate this level of understanding, ensure your questions are conceptually clear and specific. They should be short and straightforward, without any jargon. The questions must also be researchable. Your concepts must be operationalizable. If you cannot measure your concept, then how will the research questions be evaluated? It is the same as if you include an element in your building plan that is structurally unsound; it that will need to be changed before the house can be built, a question that can't be answered will have to change.

Your research questions must be narrow enough to be researched in a reasonable time frame. Your resources are limited; with enough time and money anything is possible, but you don't have unlimited time (I won't hazard a guess about your finances). Each doctoral program has a time limit. You want know how much time you have to conduct your research and finish your program. Some programs have time limits on individual coursework as well. It is one of your responsibilities to know what (if any) expiration dates exist and the consequences of those expiration dates. These deadlines exist to ensure that the content at the start of your program is still relevant and current at the end of your program, when you earn your degree. While laudable, the time constraints can add stress to the dissertation process, so stay on top of your program's requirements. You want to keep your topic narrow, but not so narrow that it becomes irrelevant to the "real world".

Your research has to include enough breadth to make a contribution to the field.

Significance of the Study

In this section, you are explaining why you should earn a doctorate for your work. Your dissertation is your entrance ticket into the *Academy*. In this section, you explain how the field will benefit from your work. When writing this section, begin with your ideas, and then, praise them. Include some of your rationale and how the research fits in the current state of the field. Why is it important now? Avoid hiding in too much text; explicitly state why your research matters in very clear language.

Definition of Terms

Clarity is important throughout your writing, but when defining terms, it is especially essential. Terms must be operationalized with very basic language. Define the term in the simplest way, grounding the definition in a reference from the field. This is not the place for a dictionary definition (no offense to Webster). Your audience may not have read the seminal works relevant to your topic, and will likely be unfamiliar with acronyms. Since you are writing about a problem that holds educational significance, ensuring that you communicate effectively will require you to reduce your use of jargon and acronyms (Gregory, 2015). Many times the definition will come from instrumentation that you are using, but in the case of less obviously attributable terms, look for definitions in the research you are reading to ground your study.

Assumptions

Like terms, any assumptions must be explicitly defined. An assumption, for the purposes of dissertation work, is a factor that may influence your study but cannot be described with empirical data. Assumptions may be looked at as self-evident truths, but even though they may appear self-evident, in dissertation research they must be explicitly stated. Look at all the ways you accessed information to establish your literature base. Did you exclude some types of information because you deemed them less trustworthy? If so, that was based on an assumption. Did you use mainly sources from one country? What about the timing of your sources? Anything that contributed to your decision-making is fair game for consideration in this section.

You may never fully know the impact of assumptions, and you either can't or don't intend to control for them. While you may not be able to control for your assumptions, you can discuss them (and possibly verify them) with anecdotal data or other sources. Unlike reliability and validity, which will be discussed in chapter three, the choice of a particular instrument may be based on assumptions about how that instrument might apply to your research setting. Additionally, the honesty of participant responses may be reported as an assumption. How can you draw conclusions from data that may be inaccurate? What can you do to encourage authentic responses to your investigation? What factors are influencing your decisions and the possible responses of your participants? Consider everything when you are describing the assumptions that underlie your research. You build your credibility as a researcher through your careful analysis of the assumptions that may impact your study.

Limitations

Limitations are minor threats to the internal or external validity of your research. Limitations are beyond your control as a researcher, but impact your research. Think of Covey's (2004) circle of influence and circle of concern, your limitations are within your circle of concern, but they are not in your circle of influence. If your limitations are too extensive, you may wish to (or even need to) change the method or purpose of your research. A limitation may be a lack of pre-existing data to support your hypotheses or the restrictions that exist in the approach chosen, i.e. correlational vs. causal-comparative research. One caveat: if there is a lack of empirical evidence to support your hypotheses, there ought to be a strong discussion of the theoretical rationale for your choices.

Another type of limitation is anything that narrows the scope of your research, but is beyond the researcher's control. For example, if the sample is only available for one week and the researcher can only gather data during this window of opportunity, this may mean that longitudinal data is impossible. It is important to identify limitations here, but the grater discussion of how the limitations affect the study's generalizability should be saved for chapter three.

Delimitations

Like limitations, delimitations impact the generalizability of the findings of your research, but unlike limitations, delimitations are the choices you make to consciously narrow your study. These are features of your study that are within your circle of influence (Covey, 2004). The setting of your research is generally a delimitation. If you are unsure as to what might be delimiting your study, think about all the design factors where you made a choice. Each of those choices may be a delimitation. You will know that it delimits your study if making a different choice would narrow your work, or expand it in some way. If your research is qualitative, you will likely have more and different delimitations than quantitative research would. Qualitative research is more about the depth of understanding, whereas quantitative research is more about the generalizability. Use the limitations and delimitations sections to clearly define the boundaries and scope of your research, just as your blueprints define the spaces within your home.

Summary

The summary acts as GPS for every chapter, orienting the reader to what he/she has seen, and what he/she will see in the future. Each university has different guidelines regarding the tense in a summary. Some schools require past tense throughout the summaries, even when the summary is referring to upcoming parts of the document. This is challenging from a logical point of view, but it is residual from academic traditions. Other schools use a shift in tense in the summary, past tense when discussing things that have already been written in the document and then future tense for the upcoming sections. Check with your university's guidelines and your dissertation committee mentor/chair/sponsor to determine which is the appropriate form.

The content of the summary is pretty general. Without citations and references, the main ideas of the chapter are summarized, and then, the overviews of each paragraph are stated. The challenge lies in doing the same thing five times (once for each chapter) and somehow keeping it interesting. This is not a job for copy/paste. The summary for chapter one will discuss chapter one in greater detail, for the other chapters the references to chapter one will be more superficial. In this way you keep the reader focused on the key elements of the study throughout the document.

So how do I know when I am done?

First, I am sorry to say you don't ever get fully done with any section. Even now, years later, if I go back into my dissertation I will find some things that I could re-write to make them stronger. That being said, you get to a point of diminishing return, and so you will reach a point where your chapter one is ready for your committee, even if it isn't done. So, step-by-step, see if you can easily answer yes to the following questions, if so, then you are likely ready to share your work with your chair/sponsor/mentor.

Criterion	Yes	Not Yet
Does your chapter one sets the stage for the entire study?	☐	☐
Does your chapter one include an introduction/ synopsis of the literature on the key variables and concepts?	☐	☐
Are acronyms and abbreviations minimized, and where used, explained?	☐	☐
Does your chapter one include a framework and your rationale for the use of this model or framework?	☐	☐
Does your chapter one position your study in relation to current events?	☐	☐
Does your chapter one situate your study in the larger field?	☐	☐
Does your chapter one establish both relevance and significance for your study?	☐	☐
Does your chapter one include a succinct problem statement?	☐	☐
Is your problem statement put into a context based on the literature?	☐	☐
Does your problem statement clearly explain why this is a problem?	☐	☐
Is your problem statement focused and clearly stated?	☐	☐
Does your chapter one contain a clear statement of the purpose?	☐	☐
Is your purpose statement derived from the problem statement?	☐	☐
Is your problem statement put into a context based on the literature?	☐	☐
Is your purpose statement clear, succinct and no longer than 1-2 paragraphs?	☐	☐
Does your chapter one establish the scope of the study?	☐	☐
Does your chapter one contain your research questions?	☐	☐
Does your chapter one include definitions of terms from the literature, not Webster?	☐	☐
Does your significance of the study establish the stated problem and place the study in the larger context of scholarly work?	☐	☐

Are your research questions explicitly connected to your study's title?	☐	☐
Do your research questions reflect an understanding of the literature?	☐	☐
Do your research questions refer to the measures used (as appropriate) with consistent references to variables/constructs?	☐	☐
Are your research questions consistently formatted for the intended method?	☐	☐
Are your limitations appropriate for the intended methodology?	☐	☐
Have you included all the potential weaknesses of your study?	☐	☐
Does your list of delimitations include all the ways in which you narrowed the scope of your research?	☐	☐

Conclusion

The first chapter of your dissertation provides a survey of the landscape and a description of the general blueprint you will follow as you conduct your research. In keeping with our metaphor, it does not include the detailed schematics and plans for framing, plumbing, and electrical, but does include enough detail so that the contractors know where to build on your plot and what type of house you are building.

All the elements of chapter one align, and all are interdependent. Terms that are defined stem from the background sources and connect directly with the way the research question(s) will be answered to address the stated problem. This being said, a change to one element of chapter one will likely generate the need for changes throughout the rest of chapter one, so time spent conceptualizing and planning is time well-spent in the initial phases. You will benefit from getting to know yourself and your own pre-dispositions as a researcher and writer before you draft any text. Rushing the initial brainstorming and planning will result in more revisions and a greater likelihood for frustration down the line.

Chapter 5: The Literature Review

The literature review, generally chapter two of your dissertation, serves as the foundation to your research. Many factors play a role in how structurally sound a foundation is. As a builder, you aim to manage all the factors that influence the foundation's quality. The forms have to be laid out in a way that is true to the plans, the concrete has to have the appropriate mix and be kept at the right level of moisture and temperature for a good cure, and you have to do whatever you can to ensure that there are no gaps or air bubbles in the pour. A foundation can't be rushed. If a foundation cracks, it requires a lot of resources (time, money) to repair it, so it is infinitely wiser to attend to the details up front.

Your literature review will take time, and will also require that you have developed a strong system of organization. I wanted to have a digital system for my research when I was writing my dissertation, but my work style left me with multi-colored pens and lots of paper. I wish I had developed a digital habit then, but I wasn't up to changing my old habits and becoming an expert in my chosen area at the same time. Avoid beating yourself up; embrace what works for you, and be consistent.

A key to a good literature review is that is can stand on its own and contribute something substantial. Too often, students string together summaries of what they read and do not critically analyze or synthesize the material. When you are reading, consider whether the same few authors are being cited over and over. If you see this, read and re-read those authors so that you will know if they are being cited appropriately. In honing your critiquing skills, heightening your awareness of when sources are being well-used versus just sprinkled in for effect is crucial. The courses you have taken in quantitative and qualitative analysis also play a key role in developing your level of critique. Did the author report an effect size in a quantitative study, or just the statistical significance? How representative was the sample? Is the sample similar to the one you intend to study? How valid and reliable is the instrument the author has chosen to use? Are the constructs or variables defined in the same way that you are defining them? For a qualitative study, how were the conclusions drawn? How were the subjects chosen? How well-aligned with the extant literature were the data gathering protocols? Your evaluation of the quality of the research you are reading is at least as important as the findings and conclusions the authors report. As you develop your critique, you will also have to determine how you want to present the literature you have reviewed.

With the analysis of the existing published literature, you create an argument for the reader. You present the review of literature in a way that minimizes bias and thoroughly explores the concepts and variables integral to your research. Your literature review can be organized in a topical format, a chronological format, or any other way that will produce a strongly-written review.

A review is just that; you look again at the material in light of the other information available. For example, *A Nation Accountable* (2008) is connected to *A Nation at Risk* (1983). How they are connected and how the educational landscape changed between their publications dates is as important as the types of evidence, style of writing, and use of rhetoric in each document. Explore each author's work in relation to the body of work in the field. It is mainly through your chapter two that you demonstrate to the reader and the academy that you are an expert in the field.

Aside: When reading articles from journals, pay close attention to the writing style. When you are nearly done with your dissertation, that month between when you have finished the text and are awaiting your defense date, break your dissertation down in to 2-3 chunks with slightly different foci. Mirror the style in the journals referenced in the study, and then approach your advisor/sponsor about publishing the work after your defense.

Theoretical Framework

Like the conceptual framework section in chapter one, the theoretical framework in chapter two grounds your research in the theory. Take time to develop how your work fits within a theoretical lens, the ontology with which you align, and how closely your work fits the theory in comparison to the work of others who have also applied it. If you are pulling from multiple theories, thoroughly explain how they fit together to gird your work. If a diagram would show these relationships, then use, modify, or create one.

While a well-described theoretical framework is the quality of the concrete for the foundation for your study, low-quality concrete, or an ill-fitting or inadequately described theoretical framework will likely crumble or collapse when you go to analyze your data. Through your theoretical framework and the rest of chapter two, you are establishing a solid base of prior research upon which your choice of research method and conclusions rest.

Take the time to fully develop all your ideas and connections here so that the work that follows will be well-supported. Concrete that is too wet or too dry won't gain appropriate strength. It is important to be explicit and use plain language, though it might be tempting to hide behind obscure vocabulary and convoluted sentence structure. To be fair, there are some programs, mentors, chairs and sponsors who are looking for erudite language as evidence that you have sufficient knowledge to be a member of the academy. Some theories are written for a very narrow, scholarly audience. This is not your audience. You may be in the situation of having to translate the theoretical work of others into a jargon-free, accessible form. "I would not give a fig for the simplicity this side of complexity, But I would give my life for the simplicity on the other side of complexity" (Oliver Wendell Holmes as cited in Lederach, 2005, p. 31). In chapter two, you aim for the simplicity on the far side of complexity.

Content Sections

In these sections you deeply explore the content of your dissertation. You will have a section for all of the main concepts or variables in your study. Think of these sections as the forms for the foundation walls. A foundation wall that is poured in a form that is too thin or too shallow will fail to support the structure. The concrete may set with sufficient hardness, but there is just not enough of it to hold up the load of the finished home. Each section, while connected to the others, must be able to stand alone. It will have a beginning, middle, and end. With these sections, you synthesize everything relevant to your study. You want to make sure that you cover the content thoroughly, but with a purpose, a design.

How you arrange the content sections of the literature review is nearly as important as making sure it is both comprehensive and up-to date. That being said, there are some traditional ways to organize your content sections: chronologically, from general to specific, or from specific to general. You do not have to use one of these formats. Take a look at all your variables or concepts. How do they flow? I don't mean to beat you over the head with it, but a concept map illustrates how your variables relate and can help you determine how you want to organize your review of the literature.

Assuming you are now on board with the idea of a concept map, when you develop your initial concept map, kitchen sink it (i.e. put everything on it, including the kitchen sink)! Once you have everything possible on your map, take a look at it. Which are the most important concepts to include in your review of the literature, and which are less important? These decisions are critical and you may wish to get opinions from your colleagues and your committee. You may also find opinions in the literature; which of these concepts do other authors frequently include, and which are excluded? If you believe that some facets of your topics are erroneously excluded in other reviews or articles, by all means include them. Take care, however, to keep your organization focused. Everything should be essential to answering your research questions. If something is not integral to understanding the study, it should be excluded, no matter how interesting.

Frequently, a concept map will lead to a very structured outline. An outline keeps the review focused and prevents repetition. A grave danger for any chapter two is digression. If it is not important enough to be a major concept in the chapter or connect to the main ideas, then it will detract from the study. Tangents are a guilty pleasure in which you cannot indulge in dissertation writing (unlike manuscripts like this). The outline begins with the ordering of the concepts from the concept map. From the ordered topics, use the propositions and connecting ideas to develop and deepen the outline. As you read more, embed supporting points and reference authors and pages directly into the outline format (figure 1). These references do not need to be in APA format, but formatted in a way that will enable you to find them later. Resist the temptation to start writing full sentences and paragraphs into your outline.

I.   Fiscal, Administrative, PD support (Birmingham, 2004-ii)

ii.   Inclusion/integration (Fashola, 2002-80f, Miller 2003-12)

     A.   Include evaluator form the beginning (Fashola 2002-80)

     B.   Include families and community (Fashola, 1998-60, Miller, 2003-10)

     C.   Fill gaps in community (Halpern, 2004)

iii.   Evaluation (Fashola, 2002-82)

     A.   Record all relevant information (Fashola, 2004-81)

     B.   Evaluation should be built in (Fashola, 1998-60, Wiggins, 1998)

Figure 1. Excerpt from a dissertation outline. Note that this is in the earlier stages of the outline; more sources were added before writing.

Your outline will likely grow to be multiple pages. Take it with you wherever you go, whenever you think you may have a chance to think about your work. If you are a pen and paper person like me, triple spacing your outline will permit ample space to write your ideas. As you read articles, literally record where supporting ideas that fit into your outline are found. Note that the outline in Figure 1 includes page references for me, so that I knew where to look to re-read before writing that section. Whether you are more structured, or less formal, the outline will serve to focus your work.

Those of you more digitally inclined may be horrified that I was writing on a hard copy each day and then every night before bed I would type what I had written into my large, desktop tower of a computer. I printed it every morning and taped it to the wall in front of me before I started reading for that day. I am slightly embarrassed by my process, but I recognize that everyone will have their own way of doing things. One student who is very technology savvy really liked the program NVivo[7] where she could "code" the different

---

[7] Here is the link to the website for NVivo:
http://www.qsrinternational.com/

56

variables and concepts in all the PDFs she was reading, and then "query" the program to pull the relevant sections she had coded when she was ready to write that section. NVivo also allowed her to write memos to herself and annotations while she was reading so that she didn't have to look around for the piece of paper with her analysis, as it was connected to the digital file.

Whether you are working in the cloud or in a notebook, keep track of all your ideas as they happen. When you begin to write (from your outline), remember that the bulk of your writing is not summaries of work that has been done by others, but a thoughtful synthesis and critique of that work. How does one study relate to the others in the field and how do those relate to our work? A common mistake that is made in writing chapter two is writing mini book reports for every article. This reads like an annotated bibliography when it is done well and in no case does it build a cohesive argument. Keeping a record of your ideas as they occur when you are reading will aid in your synthesis.

If you are not having ideas or thinking about connections when you are reading, a few things may be going on. You could be at a very early stage in your research, so hang on…it will start happening. If you have been reading a bunch of articles and are still not generating your own ideas, you may have an unfortunate habit of reading superficially. Try to change the way in which you approach an article., Read the conclusions and consider how they could have been reached and how big a sample/how much evidence you think they would need to collect in order to draw those conclusions. Then, when you read the article in full, you will be judging it against what you thought they would need to support their claims.

OK, so you are an active reader, you have been reading enough to spawn ideas, it was going great and now… nothing. Consider your mental and physical health. Basically, do a systems check. When was the last time you went for a walk? Are you tired? Are you distracted? Remember that half-reading will require that you go back and re-read, ultimately taking longer than if you were to move around, get focused and then read. Perhaps you need to shift gears? When I was tired of (or frustrated with) reading to support my development of chapter two, I read very different articles to support chapter three. For me, reading about methodology, reliability, validity, and statistical analysis restored my batteries so that I could then go back to reading more theoretical or content-based articles. Again, as with everything else, you will get to know what works for you. Please just make sure you choose a healthy strategy. Do not binge eat chips while waiting for inspiration.

As you read, the authors of the articles will make compelling arguments for why what they have written about is essential, but you are creating your own review. Your outline will help with this as you will see how the different sources fit together and you can create a picture of the existing literature for the reader. You don't have to include everything someone else thought was important, but your choices must be purposeful. Back to the concrete; if you create a form that is too difficult to fill, there will be gaps in the poured foundation. Similarly, when you are looking for articles, you will want to search in a variety of different ways to make sure that you aren't missing important sources.

Your program or university will likely have provided some supports or strategies for conducting a literature search, but here are some just in case. (I am not intending to provide a iron-clad search method here, just some helpful hints). I open up the webpage for my university's library and sign in before I conduct a search in any other way. After that, I go to Google Scholar. I like how I can import articles directly into my reference managing program[8] from Google Scholar. Once I have found a source I like in Google Scholar, I use the reference list at the end of that document, and the "Cited by" link in Google Scholar. The column on the right shows you the availability of the article to you.

Depending upon your topic, a literature search can become expensive, so maximize the free resources that are available. If you can spend some time in your university's library, using the university's network provides the greatest free access to articles. I find that when I am signed into the library's webpage or on campus, more articles are available as PDFs than when I am not logged in. Using your library's interlibrary loan service will save you money, and most universities have that system online. (Back in the day, I would bring cookies to the person who was at the interlibrary loan desk as I handed her my paper slip requesting an article. I don't know if that increased the number of articles I received, but it did seem that I got my articles faster than some of my colleagues.)

Another way to access full text articles is through networks and groups. I receive requests for full-text copies of my articles through ResearchGate (https://www.researchgate.net/) and follow authors that tend to publish in areas that interest me. When I follow an author, I receive a notification whenever they publish anything new, or upload a full-text copy of an article. This helps me stay up to date in my chosen field(s). The network includes links to co-authors, so if I am

---

[8] I am currently using the free version of Mendeley (https://www.mendeley.com/). There are lots of free or paid reference managing tools. One of my students showed me this one and while it is quirky sometimes, it has made my life easier. There is an add in for MS Word so the program manages my reference list as I write. I do have to double-check the information entered into the program, but I do that at the end of each writing day when I am out of good ideas. I can actually search for more sources through the program. I am using Mendeley to manage this document's references.

interested in one author (there are a lot of people citing this person), and I find them in ResearchGate, I will not only be able to see a list of their publications, but also a list of their top co-authors. These co-authors may also have profiles I can view and possibly follow. Finally, ResearchGate has a feature where you can answer and ask questions related to research. You can search for questions relative to your topic, or pose a new one. There is no implied guarantee that someone will answer your question, but the "reputation" score includes both how others interact with your content and your interactions with others. It encourages the answering of questions, so can be a fresh source of information, different from conventional means.

The most conventional and useful source of reference materials is the university website[9]. If you are researching a topic and feel like you keep hitting dead ends, shift your approach. Instead of looking for an article based on content or title, browse a relevant journal's table of contents. Remember when you were little, you would go to the area of the library that featured the topic of your interest and you would read the spines of the books until one title piqued your interest? This is the same idea. (I do realize that as time passes this idea of browsing the library shelves will be less popular, but hopefully everyone will have the opportunity to find a great book because it was near something else in the Dewey Decimal System.) So, check out a journal in the library's holdings because of its title and skim through the table of contents. You might serendipitously find an article that will re-energize your search!

The goal here remains to craft a comprehensive review of the literature that will support the rest of your study. At the start of the chapter I mentioned both the mix of the concrete

---

[9] The Southern Connecticut State University library, Buley Library, http://libguides.southernct.edu/home, includes many useful digital holdings as well as on campus resources such as many computers (both mac and pc) for faculty and student use, study rooms that students can book, and a coffee shop.

and the pour. The right mix of Portland cement, water and aggregate are needed for strong concrete, just as the mix of theoretical, conceptual, and empirical articles are in your review of literature. The pour refers to the speed at which you pour the concrete: if you pour the concrete too fast, you can get air bubbles and pockets in your foundation (or even bust through your form!). Some of these bubbles may be so small that they are undetectable, but other bubbles, even if they can't be seen from the exterior of the foundation walls, can leave weak spots that won't hold up under pressure.

To avoid bubbles and gaps in your foundation, use a variety of search approaches. I was told that I would know when I had conducted a thorough review of the literature when I was reading articles that cite articles I had already read. This appears to only be part of the story. A solid starting place, for certain, but blind to a possible systemic bias. If I only use Google Scholar to search, even if I am very thorough with my search terms, I am still only going to pick up articles that have been indexed by Google Scholar. If I limit my search to articles that I can access immediately for free, then I exclude all the databases to which my university has not subscribed. When building a foundation of research, you want to create the strongest base possible. Track *how* you are accessing reference materials and touch base with colleagues and your librarians to see if there are other methods that haven't yet been tried. In this way, you shake or tap the form, forcing the air bubbles out of your foundation.

Writing it Up

Now that you have read widely on your topic, you need to start writing. For some, this process provides a release, freeing them to engage with the material he or she has been reading and thinking about. Not everyone feels this way. If you fit in the former category, hooray! Most of us don't, and will experience some difficulties as we turn our elaborate outline into the written word. When you review your outline before writing, make sure it reflects the document you wish to write. The formation of your argument relies not only on the quality of information you have gathered as you read and the level of critique you offer, but how you pull everything together.

Back, once again, to the cement; a poured cement foundation won't develop its desired strength if it cures at the wrong temperature. If the concrete is too cold, the Portland cement and water don't form the crystals required to strengthen the cement, just as a review of literature that does not form an effective argument is weak. Conversely, a literature review that has too much argument will read as biased, and lose credibility. It will crack and crumble the same way a foundation poured at too high a temperature will, because it cured too fast. While you want to make your case, you make with with the research and evidence you present, rather than stating it outright. Look for a balance of evidence and argument, with the later being a function of how you organized the former.

While you are finding your balance in presenting your analysis and evidence, you also have to remain mindful of your writing style. Each section has to flow and transition. An unfortunately popular misconception is that a heading or subhead will replace a missing transition, which simply doesn't work. You will have to explicitly connect your ideas, developing logical transitions (think concept map). Here again, you are seeking to be understood; the ability to write clearly and without jargon is crucial. Remember that for a U.S. audience, the reader is not expected to have to work to understand your writing.

Lastly, remember that at the end of each chapter, you are including a note to the reader about how this chapter fits into the larger picture of the whole dissertation. With the summary for chapter two, pay special attention to wrapping up how your variables fit together and how the variables are going to be studied to address your research questions, and why answering the questions is important. This provides a smoother transition into chapter three, in which you will give the reader much more detail on how you will be answering your research questions.

Self-Assessment

One challenge with chapter two is that even as you are writing, so are others. At some point, you must stop searching for more sources and commit to what you have. That sounds like bad advice, but if you keep updating, you will never finish. Use the following questions to help you determine if you have brought your chapter two to a point where it is ready to be read by your committee.

Criterion	Yes	Not Yet
Is everything you included in your review of the literature directly related to your stated research problem and questions?	☐	☐
Is every variable and concept in your study explored in the review of literature?	☐	☐
Is your review of the literature organized into sections and subsections with appropriate headings?	☐	☐
Is the purpose of every section clear and unique from other sections?	☐	☐
Do ideas and concepts build on each other within a section?	☐	☐
Does your writing include transitions between sections and subsections?	☐	☐
Does your chapter two have its own introduction body and concluding sections?	☐	☐
Do each of your sections have their own introduction body and concluding sections?	☐	☐
Are terms and concepts used consistently?	☐	☐
Are acronyms and abbreviations minimized, and where used, explained?	☐	☐
Have you integrated the relevant seminal works in the field?	☐	☐

Have you included contemporary references?	☐	☐
Have you discussed what trends, debates, or evolutions have existed in the relevant research?	☐	☐
Have you explored the research in sufficient depth to justify instrument or protocol choices?	☐	☐
Is your literature review broad enough to include "anchors" for your analysis?	☐	☐
Does your review of the literature include a balance of both theoretical and empirical literature?	☐	☐

Conclusion

"If I have seen further, it is by standing on the shoulders of giants."[10] (Newton, 1959). In your review of the literature, you seek to demonstrate that you have integrated and critiqued the existing literature into a giant upon whose shoulders you may now stand. This chapter serves as your research's foundation, and as that supporting mass, requires great care in its formation. Through diligent and deliberate research, you craft an argument that leaves no doubt in the reader's mind that you are aware of and have deeply considered the seminal works in the field and recent developments that impact the concepts and variables in your study.

---

[10] This quote interests me on so many levels. It is appropriate as you are situating your work on the work by others, but beyond that, Newton tends to get the credit for creating Calculus. There is controversy over whether he or Gottfried Leibniz actually invented it. Also, this very quote has roots in the words of others. Newton "borrowed" the part of the phrase "on the shoulders of giants" from earlier writings. Here, too, Newton was standing on someone else's shoulders!

Chapter 6: Methodology

The title of this chapter is sometimes mislabeled research method. A research method is the data gathering plan and the data analysis plan; it is not as encompassing as a research methodology which includes the rationale and philosophical assumptions as well as the research method. As you will be discussing the *why* of your choices, this chapter's appropriate title is methodology.

Your chapter three includes the research methodology and the research methods, the why and the how. You provide a painstakingly detailed plan so that another researcher could reproduce your study. If you hand your chapter three to someone and he or she would not know how to go from point A to point B, then it requires more detail. One way to achieve this level of detail is to use your journal to track what you do as you do it. If you wait until the end of your study to record details, the tricks our memory plays will make accurate recall very difficult.

Think of your chapter three as the detailed plans, schematics, and framing. Together, these define the shape and functions of the rooms of your house, making it your home. You build the exterior walls on your foundation (Chapter 2), including the windows where they can maximize the location you have chosen on the plot of land (Chapter 1). During chapter three you need to figure out where you will need plumbing, electrical, and what type of heat so you can frame your walls appropriately. Like chapter 2, foundation work, rushing the planning of chapter three can lead to costly retrofitting.

I know that earlier in this text I mentioned that you will want to do some soul-searching to get to know yourself as a researcher, as a means of determining your ontological and epistemological stance. If you have not yet done that, there is still time! Your research will be a function of your research philosophy (O'Gorman & MacIntosh, 2015). O'Gorman & MacIntosh have written a chapter that articulates the interactions of how your reserch paradigm drives your decisions[11].

A strong chapter three is grounded in methodological resources. A non-exhaustive list of some valuable resources is in appendix B, but some of the best resources are in journals on methodology. These journals will have the most up-to-date discussions about existing methods as well as the first words on emerging methods. You can use Google Scholar and ReserchGate again here to access journal articles that explore the methods you are considering. There are also free groups that are available online such as Methodspace (http://www.methodspace.com/). Methodspace offers discussions about research methods and a space for Q & A. One caution with using a website like this (or any other site where anyone can answer or edit content, i.e. Wikis) is you must to be savvy about which advice you take. Anyone can post an answer, but a quick "Google" of the author will help you evaluate the credibility of the post.

Once you have a feel for your own philosophy and how you think you might approach your study, it is time to start

---

[11] Not only do O'Gorman & MacIntosh dedicate a full chapter to this discussion, but they have created a great picture that illustrates it (page 51). I highly recommend you download this chapter, I found it online at http://tinyurl.com/olc9lag, and the full citation is in the references.

working on the details. Remember you laid some of this out in chapter one, or alternately, part of chapter one is unfinished because you were waiting to figure this stuff out. Whatever you do in chapter three, make sure that chapter one is updated so that you are consistent throughout your document.

Research Design

It may seem like splitting hairs to have an introductory section, a research design section, and a research method section. They serve different purposes; the introductory section will give the overview (plans, layout, how many rooms/baths), the research design will set the research in its place within the field of research in general (big decisions like how you will heat the house) and the research method will outline how the research was conducted (detailed schematics and framing). If you keep the goals of each section clear, then it will not be overly repetitious, but rather like observing the same research through different lenses. Each will bring something fresh and unique to the project.

How you design your research stems from your research philosophy, problem statement, and your research questions. Your research questions hold the whole project together. Your research design will ensure that you collect evidence allowing you to answer the research questions as clearly as possible. There are a multitude of research designs and each of those can be combined in a myriad of ways. Initially, you will want to determine whether you are conducting an experimental, quasi-experimental, or non-experimental study. If you are in control of assigning groups (rarely the case in educational research) and you choose a random assignment of groups, you are conducting an experimental study. If the groups are pre-assigned (like students grouped in classrooms) but you can determine whether the group is a control or a part of the treatment group, then you have a quasi-experimental study. If you cannot establish a control, you have a non-experimental study.

Once you have classified your study this way, it is time to determine the type of data you are looking to collect. Are you seeking mainly numerical data, like Likert scale responses or test scores? If this is the case, you are conducting a quantitative (QUAN) study. If, on the other hand, your data are more verbal or written, then your research is more qualitative (QUAL). For years, researchers have pulled from both of these models to improve their research. If both forms of data are analyzed together, this is called a mixed methods study and may have several possible formats.

The two most common forms of mixed methods designs are the embedded and sequential designs. In the embedded mixed method design, both the qualitative and quantitative data are collected at the same time (or close to the same time). Depending on which of the two is dominating the research the embedded design may be described as either [QUAL(quan)] or [QUAN(qual)]. In a sequential mixed methods study, the qualitative and quantitative data collection efforts are in a pre-determined order, and data analysis from the first method are used to shape the following method. There is no limit to the number of data collection episodes, but the earlier data collection must influence the later. If the early data are not informing the later data collection efforts, it is not truly sequential, and would be better described as embedded.

Other types of research design may include both qualitative and quantitative data, but if the data are not analyzed together to support each type of finding, they are not true mixed- methods designs. The merging of the analyses is what classifies a method as mixed. An example of this might be a longitudinal, case study, or a cross-sectional design. In all these methods you may collect both quantitative and qualitative data, but in the longitudinal, case study, and cross-sectional designs the data may be treated separately, and would therefore not be considered mixed methods.

Like the rest of your document, your research design should be grounded in sources. There are some authors who are commonly cited for each type of research design; read journal articles and dissertations that have used your anticipated design to determine the key players for your intended design. Use those resources as a primer and find the seminal works and authors for describing your chosen research design. Your committee will likely be familiar with the authors you will referencing, so be sure to have read the author's original work (of course you would do this anyway, it is just key to not use the "as cited in" approach when supporting your research design). Also, many texts purport to be authorities in research design and research methods, please use the secondary sources (like textbooks) as supplemental. Seek primary sources. For example, John Creswell has written a number of books on research design (Creswell & Clark, 2011; Creswell, 1994, 2014), but he has also written journal articles on design and methods (Creswell & Garrett, 2008; Creswell & Miller, 2000). While the texts may have been where you first read about a design, the journal article is a preferred source. Go ahead and cite both!

Research Methods

Once you have decided on your research design, then it is time to look at the methods for your research. The methods are the actual plans for data collection, the *how*. Will you be using a survey or questionnaire? What about an interview? If you are using an interview, will it be structured or more loosely structured? For an interview or focus group, how was the protocol developed? How will the data be analyzed? These very specific, nuts and bolts questions are your research methods. These too should be supported with references. This section is a recipe for your research; it should be written with such painstaking detail that it could be replicated.

Context

The context of your research helps the reader understand the setting in which your research takes place. The challenge here is to provide enough information to the reader without identifying the exact setting for confidentiality. Your study exists in a political and organizational context that may have dimensions beyond those that are apparent to you now. Even if the setting is granting permission to conduct the research, their identity should be protected in your dissertation. For example, if you are using Strategic School Profile data to describe the setting, use rounded numbers to describe the population or ranges, such as "over 95% of students receive free or reduced lunch" instead of the actual number (95.7% or a slightly rounded 96%).

Similarly, you will provide pseudonyms for schools and individuals. Since your goal is to protect the participants in your research, aim to keep the pseudonyms generic. It is tempting to provide pseudonyms that amuse you, for example, for Lincoln Elementary you might choose John Wilkes Booth Elementary. While this is witty, it actually reduces the level of confidentiality. Perhaps a reader is familiar with the area and reads the description of John Wilkes Booth Elementary, because Booth and Lincoln are associated in history, the reader is more likely to identify Lincoln Elementary. It would be better to choose a very different name if you are sticking with a name, like Neil Armstrong Elementary, or better still something totally unrelated, Maple Elementary.

Other concerns I have with the application of pseudonyms are not related to witty choices by the researcher. There are times when the protection of confidentiality is at odds with the wishes of the research participant, or the requirements of mandated reporting (Grinyer, 2002; Lahman et al., 2015; Wiles, Crow, Heath, & Charles, 2008). Less explicitly, a researcher can introduce a bias, either subconsciously or purposefully, that impacts the reporting or reading of the research. In an effort to include multicultural names, a researcher, knowing the participants and their responses, then must assign different characteristics to the cultures. The inclusive intent of the researcher then leads to challenges of implicit biases and confronting biases.

The researcher choosing pseudonyms always introduces another level of choice for the researcher and it is not one to take lightly. Using non-name pseudonyms decreases the bias stemming from researcher selected names, but increases the level of distance between the reader of the research and the data; an undesirable consequence in qualitative data reporting when you want the reader to get a feel for the experience of the participant. Grinyer (2002) suggests allowing the research participant to choose his/her own pseudonym, but warns that can lead to duplications. Perhaps a solution would be to ask the participant to chose a few possible pseudonyms. As the researcher, you will have to determine how you navigate this morass, and explain your choice.

Sample

Similar to the context of the study, the sample should be depicted with sufficient detail to inform the reader without so much detail that the participants are identifiable. If you are conducting research in the district in which you work, take exceptional care in protecting the district. Every researcher has a digital footprint, and that footprint includes your work history. To circumvent this challenge, you may wish to seek permission from several similar schools, districts, or organizations, and include a description that could work for all of them in your document. The letters of support that permit you to conduct your research will be in your appendices, but the data will be unidentifiable. If you have permission from three or four sites and something doesn't work with the first site where you collect data, you now have backup plans already in place.

Describing the sample and protecting confidentiality is a balancing act which may require you to seek trusted peers for feedback. Give them your description of the sample and ask them if they can identify the group you are studying. When it has passed this level of scrutiny, seek advice from your committee. Save the committee for a final check, or if you need approval on a decision you are making. It bears repeating: the more structured you are in your communication, the more help you will get as a response to your query.

Data Gathering Plan

Your data gathering plan is even more detailed in your research method section. Here, you will identify every step in collecting your data. To some, this level of detail will seem tedious, but it helps the reader understand what level of confidence they should have in your data and your research in general. If you contacted someone to secure access to the research population, record the date that their letter was sent, append the inquiry letter, record the date of the response, and append the permission letter. You may need to redact the names and/or e-mail addresses in the appendices; an easy way to do that is to scan the document, then place a white rectangle over the identifying information. In this way, you maintain the integrity of the original document, but can include the redacted version in your dissertation.

Other things to include in the data gathering plan are the IRB permission, the permission to use a survey or questionnaire, and any other permissions and procedures. This section will act like external memory of your data collection process. If you are collecting data online, when was the invitation to participate sent, were reminders sent, when was data collection closed? Another thing to consider is how the choices you make can be justified. If you close a survey after fourteen days, explain why fourteen days was chosen and support that with references.

72

As you are documenting the data gathering process, consider what else you could have done. When you initially designed your research you delimited your study; were there things that came up since then that required you to make choices to keep your study focused? Some of these might be appropriately placed in your delimitations, while others may be used in chapter five when you discuss future research. There is no way to anticipate every choice you will have to make when you initially conceive your study, but through diligent record-keeping, you can account for all the choices you make in your study.

Quantitative Data

Another aspect of diligent record-keeping is data management. When you are working with any data, it is imperative that you have a plan for managing your data, securing it, working with it, and storing it after your research is completed. When you are working with quantitative data, you will need to specify which program you will be using to analyze your data. The statistical program for the social sciences (SPSS) is commonly used, but some researchers are starting to use the open source R language and environment for statistical analyses. Discuss any data analysis program choice with your committee. Also, consider the amount of support you may need and the availability of that support depending on the software you choose for your analyses. If you stray from the convention, you will likely want to include a discussion justifying your choice in your dissertation.

Qualitative Data

Qualitative data requires the same, if not more, diligence regarding data management. Qualitative research may include vast amounts of data in the form of transcriptions, interview recordings, open-ended responses, observation logs, documents, or other forms of written records. Not only do these need to be managed, but the notes and comments on these also need to be handled. In keeping with the computing available for working with quantitative data, there are several programs available for working with such data. A choice of program is not the same as an analysis plan, which I will discuss next. Programs such as TAMS[12], NVivo[13] and ATLAS.ti[14] are popular for analyzing and organizing qualitative data. These programs allow you to keep your notes and ideas (memos or annotations) in the same project file as your data. Qualitative data were managed and analyzed before computers and programs, and while helpful, computer programs are not required for qualitative research.

Data Analysis Plan

This section describes how you will use the data you have collected to address your research questions. Not surprisingly, a mistake here can derail your research, but unlike earlier snafus that can be devastating, since you collected the data with fidelity, a mistake here can be rectified quite easily. To be perfectly honest, many people "play" with their data once it is collected to see what is there. Just because you develop and describe a data analysis plan before you collect your data does not mean that the proposed analyses are the only ones that can be applied to your data once collected.

Even though you may later add other approaches, both qualitative and quantitative data require thick description regarding how the data will be analyzed that is both appropriate for the research questions and supported by relevant sources. The how, when, and why of your data analysis plan is crucial. If you can't describe how your data analysis plan will answer

---

[12] TAMS, Text Analysis Markup System, is a free program designed for ethnographic and discourse research. http://tamsys.sourceforge.net/

[13] NVivo is a paid program for either mac or PC http://tamsys.sourceforge.net/ there is a 14-day trial available.

[14] ATLAS.ti, another paid program is available for PC, mac or mobile. http://atlasti.com/product/ there is a trial versions of the mac and PC format that is not limited by time, but rather by size.

your research questions, then one or both will need to change. Remember that if you make a change here in chapter three, you may have to go back and update chapter one to be consistent. It is not a big deal to make the changes; it is, however, a big deal if you are inconsistent.

A common mistake in data analysis is describing the tool that will be used rather than how the tool will be used. For example, qualitative research may be analyzed using ATLAS.ti, but how the researcher will use ATLAS.ti needs to be explained. Will the researcher use *a priori* codes, emergent codes, document memos, or another plan to find the meaning within the data? If a researcher is using SPSS to analyze his/her quantitative data, is the researcher using a correlational technique or a form of regression? The justifications for the choices made here are based not only on the research questions and design, but also in the body of literature.

A researcher can pay a professional for data analysis, but this comes with inherent challenges. The researcher is the one that conceived the study; the consultant can only do what the researcher asks, and, at that point, it may not be worth the money. If a researcher deems that it is worth the expense, they must take careful notes, as the consultant will not be at the defense to explain the analyses. The researcher is responsible for presenting the data and the results that stem from those data. The researcher, not the consultant, is earning the degree and must answer any questions. As a professor and coach, I do not recommend hiring a consultant, but they do exist.

A final thought on the data analysis plan: remember that your reader is not the expert on your research, you are. Take time to explain any procedures used and why they are appropriate for this study. Secondary sources, such as texts, may be very useful in this section, but avoid quotes. Find *your* way of detailing your procedures and then credit the original source of the ideas contained in your words. Remember, if you have seen the same information in several texts, like a math equation, it is likely part of the common body of knowledge and therefore not attributable to any one source (*Publication Manual of the American Psychological Association*, 2009, p. 169). This is a challenge in that you have to find it in multiple sources to confirm this, and not sources citing the same original source. The Internet is helpful for this purpose, but be wary, as it full of suspect information. Take care to choose only the most reliable information as you detail your data analysis plan, and for the rest of your document.

Limitations / Delimitations

In chapter one, the limitations and delimitations were introduced. Now, in chapter three, each of the limitations and delimitations mentioned in chapter one are fully explored. Look at each limitation and delimitation and how it may impact your study. Are there studies similar to yours that have similar limitations and delimitations? Specifically for the delimitations: why have you chosen to narrow your work this way? It is key to understanding the study as a whole to understand how you conceived it, and narrowed your scope.

This section is not for excuses. This is a discussion of your choices as a researcher. Each choice has a consequence, identifying and exploring these consequences is integral to the readers' understanding of your work. It is like choosing to have eight foot ceilings in your house instead of eleven. While eleven foot ceilings are grand, if the house is located in New England, a room with eleven foot ceilings is more expensive and more difficult to heat. You are the researcher; you make the decisions that bound your study, and you have to justify and explain them.

The limitations are a little different. You didn't make the choice that limited your study due to a limitation. Perhaps the student demographic data from the district is only collected in October when it is sent to the government. Therefore, students entering the school after October may not have demographic data that has been verified by the district. If the demographic data includes variables you are studying, then students that enter after October will be excluded from your sample. Consider how this may impact your results. Does this traditionally affect a high percentage of students in the school? Does it disproportionally affect one or more subgroup(s)? Will this influence the results of the research? If so, is there a way to gather the information directly? Look at each limitation and consider its impact. While the limitation is outside your circle of influence (Covey, 2004), it is important to address how it impacts your work.

Self-Assessment

A real challenge in pulling this section of your dissertation together stems from balancing the comfort you and your committee members have with particular methods, the underlying and possibly unidentified ontologies, and epistemologies of committee members, as well as the nature of your research questions. Consequently, you can't challenge your committee's beliefs, but you can be explicit about yours and how it drives your decisions for your research.

Beyond that, here are some questions that will help you evaluate whether you have a draft of chapter three that is ready for your committee.

Criterion	Yes	Not Yet
Have you included a detailed description of your methodology and why it is appropriate for this study?	☐	☐
Is the rationale for your methodology supported by appropriate references?	☐	☐
Do the methods you have chosen align with your methodology?	☐	☐
Will the methods you have chosen provide sufficient data to answer your research questions?	☐	☐
For each method of data collection have you provided a detailed description and rationale?	☐	☐
If you are using a mixed methods design, is there a balanced treatment of both the qualitative and quantitative?	☐	☐

Does your chapter include a detailed description of your sample and how you will get access to the sample?	☐	☐
Is the sampling strategy appropriate for the methods of the study, and have you presented a supported rationale to demonstrate this?	☐	☐
Have you described the population of the study (from which your sample is drawn)?	☐	☐
For your protocols or instruments, have you included them as appendices and in the text of the chapter discussed validity, reliability, etc.?	☐	☐
Have you provided a detailed (reproducible) data-gathering plan?	☐	☐
Does your data-gathering plan include the steps of how, when, and who will collect the data?	☐	☐
Have you discussed how data will be analyzed (supported by references) including the who, when, and how they will be analyzed?	☐	☐
Does your chapter include a discussion of how confidentiality of subjects will be maintained?	☐	☐
Have you included your Institutional Review Board permission as an appendix?	☐	☐
Do you need letters of support from participating districts, schools or organizations? If so, are they included as appendices?	☐	☐

Conclusion

Your third chapter holds the detailed plans for how your research will be conducted; in other words, how your house will be built. You frame your data collection and data analysis the way you frame walls and plan for outlets. Even after you have crafted your chapter, there is some flexibility to move outlets a little, but the deeper you go into your project, the more cumbersome changes become. Every change has a cost associated with it, but some are worth it! Perhaps you had not considered adding an outlet inside the medicine cabinet in the bathroom, but then realized that you don't want your electric toothbrush on the vanity. Adding an outlet in the cabinet may cost a little extra, but you will have customized the bathroom to meet your specific needs.

If you failed to consider the electric toothbrush when you were planning, and the bathroom walls were finished, then you have a few options, you can have the cord hang from the cabinet to the outlet (unsightly!), have the toothbrush sit on the sink with the cord running to the outlet (ugh!), or switch to a manual toothbrush (just kidding!). Alternately, you can rip out the installed cabinet, possibly some more of the wall, fish electrical and install the outlet after the fact. From this, admittedly silly example, you can see that flexibility and forethought when planning the early chapters of your work can save you from extra work down the road.

Chapter 7: The Full Proposal & IRB

Whew! You have chapters one, two, and three drafted. AWESOME! You and your committee will now set a date and time for the first public viewing of your work. The proposal hearing or presentation is similar to calling for the inspector to come before you close up the walls. Calling the inspector can be scary. You want the inspector to look closely, but at the same time, you don't want the inspector to find anything big that needs fixing. This is an emotional time for you and your work. You have labored hard to get to this point, and opening your work up to the eyes of others makes you vulnerable.

Remember: you are not your work. Throughout your doctoral program, you have been getting informal feedback from colleagues, more formal critique from professors and now committee members, all of which has been filtered through your own view of your capability. When you received negative feedback, you were able to use it to improve your work, and positive feedback reinforced modifications you have made (Kolb, 1976). I have just described a healthy relationship with critique and self-esteem, but there are less productive orientations toward feedback that impede an individual's ability to productively use feedback (Anseel, Lievens, & Levy, 2007; London & Smither, 2002). When an individual connects the feedback to his or her self-image, superfluous positive feedback is sought to bolster self-esteem, and conversely, negative feedback is rejected (London & Smither, 2002). Separating your work from your sense of self creates a healthier focus on feedback; shifting the anxiety producing element of the proposal-sharing to a growth-focused orientation (Dweck, 2006; Langer, 1997).

Maintaining a growth mindset means that you will seek to have the most critical eyes on your work, and be motivated to use their feedback to improve it (Dweck, Chiu, & Hong, 1995; Fishbach & Choi, 2012). You will want to consider who might be able to provide big-picture feedback at this critical juncture. You have not yet started collecting your data, so at this point, everything is subject to modification. Consider sending a personal invitation, either by email, note, or in person, to professors you have had that have provided sophisticated critique in the past. You are inviting someone to see a brief synopsis of your work up to this point, so you want to invite people with the relevant background to ask good questions and challenge your thinking.

Your committee has read the full proposal, so their questions will encompass a deeper level of detail, but they also have been with you throughout the process. They do not have fresh eyes. You don't ask the contractor who framed the walls to evaluate how well the walls have been framed; you ask the city's building inspector.

Each program will have slightly different requirements for a proposal hearing. In general, you will have about twenty minutes to share your entire project to this point. It will be tempting to focus mainly on all the work you did to craft a comprehensive review of the literature, but that is a tactical error. Take a cue from peer-reviewed articles and keep a balance between the elements of chapters one through three. So, since there are some similar elements in chapters one and three, those will be emphasized in the presentation, as would any overviews of how you organized the review of literature more than the details of all the research you integrated into the literature review.

With your mentor, consider attending one or more proposal presentations or hearings well in advance of your own.. After the presentation, discuss the balance of the presentation with your mentor to make sure that you have a common understanding of expectations before you start pulling together materials for your proposal hearing.

Okay, so you have invited some people and have figured out that you are including elements of all the chapters one through three in one twenty-minute presentation. Alas, you can't speed talk your way through this. Some of your hard work will not be shared in the presentation. Think about how you can maximize your time. Your concept map, streamlined, might serve you well as a graphical representation of your thinking and demonstrate the concepts within your study. Graphics are very powerful in a presentation as there is insufficient time to have attendees read your proposal, and you want to solicit the most feedback possible.

Handouts which include your title, problem statement, theoretical or conceptual framework, purpose statement, research questions and your methodology and methods will give the audience a tangible organizer upon which they can jot down notes. If you are choosing to use PowerPoint or a similar program, the audience will generally expect to receive a handout with your slides, as well as room for note-taking and questions. You may also wish to include copies of your appendices and any graphics you include on your slides. Depending on how much you are already providing your audience, you may want to incorporate a copy of your reference list in your handouts. Finally, supply a table illustrating how each of your research questions will be addressed with your data sources and data analysis plan will help the audience see that you have thoughtfully considered how your research will be carried out.

Providing these materials for your audience mirrors taking the building inspector on a tour of the construction site that will be your future home. While there will always be some anxiety, you can be proud of the work you have already completed, even as you know there is more to be done. Present the materials to your audience in a polished format. Folders can help you organize the handouts in a way that is appealing and inexpensive. You can control the order in which audience members look at your work with fasteners like clips and staples. A fancier and still not more than about $25[15] option is to have a company like Staples print and bind your handouts. With professional binding, you have pre-determined the way your audience will see your work. Some schools and libraries also offer different types of binding service; ask around to see if you can have it done for free before you pay a company, if you decide to go this route.

The Proposal Hearing or Presentation

With your presentation and handouts prepared for your audience, the next step is to make sure you, yourself, are prepared. Do take the time to use the technology you will use during your presentation. Avoid using a different computer if you can manage it. Try to practice in the space you will be using, whether it is a classroom, a conference room, a meeting room, or an auditorium. Get a feel for how much you will be able to move around and what sort of view your audience will have. Determine if the room will allow you to bring in water and snacks, or if that is not permitted. You don't want to spend time and money bringing refreshments if you can't share them with your audience!

Your audience will provide you with non-verbal communication throughout your presentation; look for it and attend to it. Either edit (speed up) spots that appear to drag, or be ready to dive deeper into areas of interest. Remember, you only have twenty minutes or so, but you want to ensure the audience gets what they need to maximize feedback. If you

---

[15] In August of 2016, ten copies of a twenty-page, double sided, black and white document printed as a booklet was $21.50 at http://www.officedepot.com and $24.10 at http://documents.staples.com before the 25% off coupon.

include a card or sheet of paper with your handouts specifying that it is to be given to you at the conclusion of the presentation with feedback, questions, and thoughts, you may get the audience members to take some of your notes for you.

At the close of your presentation, you will generally ask the committee and audience members for questions. I recommend writing down every question that is asked, or asking the audience if you can audio record the question portion of the presentation. When you are in the moment, you will likely be seeking to answer the questions rather than recording them for future reflection. Since your goal in the proposal hearing is to gather feedback, documenting the questions is crucial. Perhaps you have a trusted colleague who would be willing to come to the proposal presentation and record the questions.

Since the questions come from both committee members who have read your full proposal and audience members that have only seen your presentation, the level of questions will vary widely. Audience members may ask questions that are answered in the document; take care with how you respond to these. It is better to not reference the document and just answer the question. Don't say "I included that in the written proposal." Sure you included it, but the audience member didn't get access to it, so go ahead and answer the question.

Of course there may be questions you and your committee had not considered, and that is both the goal and fear with a public proposal presentation. You want the questions that extend your thinking, and they may cause you to reconsider some of the directions you have already chosen for your research. If the question raises a great idea, but it is beyond the scope of your study, thank the questioner and gently explain this. If it has not been made clear in your delimitations section already, you will want to revise your delimitations to make it clear.

Everything in the proposal hearing is about giving you more information to revise and refine what you have already done. After the hearing, and after you have a chance to decompress, think about all the questions that were asked. Were they centered on a single chapter? If so, perhaps the way that material was presented in the presentation or handouts was unclear. Did audience members offer new references and authors to investigate? Start reading those before you get too far into making suggested edits or revising chunks of your proposal. A super new source can shake up your thinking and provide you insights that you will want to include in your chapters, perhaps even rethinking how you have some sections organized. Stay open to possibilities and maintain your growth mindset (Dweck, 2006; Langer & Moldoveanu, 2000; Langer, 1997). It is also time to shift the tense of your dissertation. As a proposal, it was mainly in the future tense, what you propose to do. Now you are working on the dissertation proper, which is a reporting of what was done, and therefore, should be framed in the past tense.

As you reflect on the ideas and questions generated during the proposal hearing, you firm up the ideas your proposed with chapters one, two, and three. They may be revised and reshaped, but you are moving forward toward data collection. This is like making your house weather-tight with a good roof and house-wrap. Your inspections went well and now it is time to start closing it up.

The Institutional Review Board, or IRB

The Institutional Review Board (IRB) safeguards against unethical research practices. Ideally, there would be no need for any oversight, but history has demonstrated otherwise. The National Institute of Health offers an online training course in Protecting Human Research Participants[16]. This course includes seven sections to be read with four of the sections having quizzes that must be passed. Part of the training includes the historically-based rationale for the IRB.

Once you have passed the training (note: you can do this any time, you don't have to wait for your proposal to be done), then you can begin to apply for IRB approval for your research. Some programs require you to have secured IRB approval before your proposal hearing, and others recommend you wait until after the hearing in case your methods change. Check with your program's documentation to ensure you are following their guidelines.

The IRB application requests similar information to what exists in your first three chapters, but much more streamlined. Please summarize rather than copy and paste. The elements that tend to slow researchers down are those that require letters from outside agencies acknowledging that you will be welcome to conduct your research at that site. When you are considering a site for data collection, ask for a formal letter that states that you will be permitted to collect data there. These letters are not only included in your IRB application, but they are also included in your dissertation as appendices.

Another sticking point in the IRB application process is the creation of consent documents. The challenge in educational research is that you may need to have a consent document for parents and a separate one for children. The document's reading level has to be consistent with the age and education level of the recipient, and there are elements that must be included in the document. The combination of these elements can offer a challenge. In MS Word, in the Tools menu offers a "Spelling and Grammar" tool where you can

---

[16] The course can be found at https://phrp.nihtraining.com and when you complete the Web-based training course you earn a printable certificate that you will include with your IRB application.

open the "options" and then click the box that measures the "readability statistics." When you run the Spelling and Grammar check, at the end, it will provide you the Flesch-Kincaid reading level. For a general, adult audience, the recommended Flesch-Kincaid reading level is 8.0.

Once you have IRB approval for your study, you can start to collect data, but you cannot make changes to your methods without completing an IRB modification form. This is why some programs request that students wait until after the proposal hearing to seek IRB approval, so they don't have to complete the additional paperwork for the modification. At the conclusion of your research, you will also complete a form for the IRB acknowledging that data collection has been completed.

Self-Assessment

The earlier self-assessments in this document serve as a checklist for you before you share some work with your committee; this one relates more specifically to you. It will help you determine if you are ready for the proposal presentation after you and your committee have determined that your draft of your proposal is ready. A good rule of thumb is to give yourself three weeks between the date that the committee has agreed that your document is ready for a public hearing or presentation and the actual date of your presentation.

Once the committee has agreed that it is time for the proposal hearing, stop editing the document. You are presenting the document that your committee has read. After the proposal has been presented you will make more changes. If you see a typo while you are preparing your presentation, flag it with a sticky note or highlight it, but leave it be. The rationale for this stems from the outcome of the proposal hearing. You will receive feedback at the hearing that is tied to page numbers. If you have edited the document, using that feedback becomes a treasure hunt.

One more suggestion along those lines, implement changes from the end of your document and then move towards the beginning. Again, shifting pagination will make using comments tied to earlier drafts more difficult. By making the changes at the end of the draft first, the location of the edits earlier in the document will not have been moved.

So, use this assessment as a tool to ease your mind as the date of your proposal hearing or presentation approaches.

Criterion	Yes	Not Yet
Has your committee had the full proposal for at least three weeks?	☐	☐
Did your document include a table of contents, list of tables and list of figures?	☐	☐
Have you checked that you have a 1:1 relationship between sources in the document and sources in your reference list?	☐	☐
Is your reference list in alphabetical order?	☐	☐
Are your appendices in the order in which they are referenced in the document?	☐	☐
Have you scouted the room in which you will present your work?	☐	☐
Have you checked (and tried) the technology in the room in which you will be presenting?	☐	☐
Have you timed your presentation and it is no longer than 20 minutes (or the time set by your program)?	☐	☐
Have you invited people who can offer you substantive feedback?	☐	☐
Have you prepared handouts for the audience that include the key elements of your study and any graphics, models, tables or figures?	☐	☐
Do you want to solicit any written comments or questions, and if so, have you provided a mechanism for that?	☐	☐
If you want to audio record the questions, do you have the tool(s) to do that?	☐	☐
If you want to have someone taking notes for you during the questions, have you asked that person?	☐	☐
Are you emotionally ready for other people to see your	☐	☐

work?

Do you have a couple phrases ready that will help you stall if you need time, or respectfully need to say you hadn't considered that idea?	☐	☐
Have you completed the NIH training?	☐	☐
Have you referred to the IRB in chapter three and can include the NIH certificate as an appendix?	☐	☐
If your program requires IRB approval in advance of the hearing, have you received approval?	☐	☐
Do you have letters stating you can collect data at the settings you have chosen for your study?	☐	☐

Conclusion

The proposal hearing and IRB are safeguards implemented as a response to research that has not gone well in the past. Imagine that you have invested all this time in planning a project, only to find out that the method you proposed will never get you the data you need to address your problem. The more eyes you have on your work belonging to those who care about your success, the better.

The building inspector will not let you slide on shoddy construction, just as a building in danger of collapsing is a public hazard. Your committee does everything it can to support you, but it takes more eyes to ensure that everything is seen. By drawing a public audience that has an interest in your topic, you open yourself up to critique, and in this way, can strengthen your work from considering the questions and issues raised by the larger group.

Once you have collected all the feedback you can at this point, then you start to close up the house, addressing issues to make it weatherproof. Aim to maintain a growth mindset and appreciate that every comment and question offered is intended to help you produce the best possible product. Everyone wants you to succeed in achieving your goal, earning your degree. With the approval of your committee and the IRB, you are ready to collect data, and begin the work on the inside of your home.

To recap, you have surveyed the whole landscape of your field and chosen an area and a specific problem to research. You have proposed a plan for that research and have become an expert in your chosen field. Then, you clearly mapped out and framed how you intend to investigate your stated problem. Finally, you have publically shared your intended work with knowledgeable others to learn from them how you can make your study even better. This has already been a long process, but now that you have earned your Department's and the IRB's approval, you are onto the last portions of this undertaking: conducting your study, reporting the results and drawing your conclusions. Please take time to appreciate what you have accomplished along the way; you only get to complete your doctoral studies once.

Chapter 8: Reporting Results

You are ready to conduct your study. That is great! It is also scary. Ideally, nothing will go wrong, and you will get exactly the data you are expecting with ease, but this is rarely the case[17]. Research, especially research worth doing, is messy. You created a plan in your proposal, but sometimes plans have to be modified. If it is a change that impacts how you collect your data, remember to have it approved by the IRB. Sometimes, once you get your first bits of data, you realize you asked the wrong questions to answer your research question.

I remember a student sought to collect data from educational leaders which met certain criteria. Unfortunately, very few of them returned his survey. He was devastated because he had intended to run statistical analyses on the results of the survey. His committee chair (not me, in case you were wondering) wisely suggested he think about what he was really interested in knowing, and whether there was another way to approach it, perhaps qualitatively. The student reconceived his work, modified his IRB to include an interview protocol, and reached out to the survey respondents. They

---

[17] If you ever took physics you know what I mean by a perfect situation. Endless problems with point masses and inelastic collisions that illustrate the mathematical models used in Physics, but only approximate what goes on in the real world, in which objects have mass and collisions involve lots of energy being converted to heat, sound, and other messy constructs. If you never took physics, once you have your doctorate, I recommend it!

were willing to be interviewed and the student gathered enough data to not only complete his dissertation and earn the degree, but also present his findings at a research conference.

I am not telling you this story to scare you, but even meticulously crafted plans don't always turn out as we expect. The aforementioned student demonstrated a strong resilience; he didn't give up. He also managed to maintain a mindset that was open to feedback and suggestion. He ended up making very significant changes to his first three chapters, even after his proposal hearing. Your document isn't ever "done" until it is signed by every member of your committee, and even then, I wager you can find something to tweak to make it better.

As you are conducting your research, it is like hiring the subcontractors to work on the inside of your home. You are making decisions every step of the way and ensuring that the work is proceeding according to the plans you have laid out. Any deviation from the plans must be sanctioned by you, and if it requires inspection, may need to be approved by your committee and possibly the IRB. You can not add an extra bathroom to your house without getting the plans and rough-ins inspected again.

Data collection can be a very exciting time. It can also be maddening, time-consuming, and lonely. You may learn a very juicy bit of information and not be able to share it due to confidentiality constraints. You may find something unexpected and have to add a content section to chapter two. You just don't know until you are in the middle of it. That's why it is a good idea to start some of your preliminary data analyses as soon as you have collected the first bits of your data. If you put up the drywall and the closet you have planned is too narrow to hold a hangar, then you need to adjust the framing before you finish drywalling and painting the whole house.

Organizing your Findings

Your chapter four, like the other chapters, requires an introduction that tells the reader what to expect. According to APA guidelines, the introductory sections don't get a header the way other sections do, but as always, follow your program's specifications. Think about the content that will be presented in this chapter; you are sharing with the world what you found in your data. You want to create an organization for your data that makes an argument from which you will draw conclusions in the next chapter. Generally, you will present your findings organized by your research questions.

You presented your research questions in chapter one and again in chapter three. You will use them here in chapter four as the guiding force for how your data are presented and ultimately used. At the start of a section where the data relevant to the research question are presented, restate both the research question and any relevant research hypotheses. This will clarify for the reader which presented data are relevant for which question or hypothesis.

Depending on the type of data you collected, presenting it may pose some logistical challenges. You will be making decisions about how you can best present your data for clarity and for ease of application to your research questions. A knowledgeable friend can be a huge help at this time; what is clear to you may not be clear to someone else. Both qualitative and quantitative data may become muddied as you divvy them up by research question. You may want to include an overview of the data before separating it out by research question. The separation of data in this manner is artificial, and a convention that is useful only for the evaluation of the stated research questions. To give the reader the big picture view, you may need to present it as the big picture first.

Once you have oriented the reader, you can more easily disaggregate your data by research question and hypothesis. Remember that the reader expects you to present the data in an easily digestible format, which may require repeating key pieces of data. If the data are presented in a table or figure, be sure that you reference the table or figure in your text, but do not repeat all the information contained in the table or figure in the text. If you repeat everything in text, what is the purpose of the figure or table? Also, ensure you have placed the figure or table as close as you can to its text reference, but not before it.

Formatting tables is governed by APA, but can frustrate even the most seasoned word processor. Appreciate that many people before you have sworn at their computers (or typewriters) when a table breaks awkwardly across two pages. If you find yourself in the unfortunate situation of having to report an overly long table, please consider the ease of the reader. Repeat the table's header on every page with the inclusion of the indication "cont." This simple gesture will be appreciated by everyone who reads your work.

Another feature of your writing that will facilitate its delivery is your use of transitions and transitional phrases. Too often in chapter four, authors forget the rules that govern good writing. Instead of transitions, some authors merely list their research question. While you do want to repeat the relevant question or hypothesis, these elements do not substitute for sufficient narration.

A massive challenge in the writing and organization of chapter four is to not include any conclusions. As you write your results, you will naturally be drawing conclusions but you can't include them in chapter four. The best suggestion I can offer is to have a separate document open (or a notebook) and record the data you are considering in chapter four and what you think it means in that separate file. Alternately, you can use the comment feature in MS word and insert a comment at the relevant information in chapter four, so you know what you were thinking when you go to write chapter five.

Expectations for Quantitative Results

If you have conducted a quantitative or mixed methods study, you will have statistical analyses to present. In chapter three, you made your case for how you were going to analyze your data; now you must enact that plan with fidelity. First, ensure that the assumptions for your intended analyses have been met. You will want to report these in a section that is independent of a research question unless these analyses are particular to only a single research question.

Also, provide a statistical description of your sample in comparison to the larger population from which it is derived and to the population it is intended to represent. If there are outliers in your sample, describe them and whether they have been included or excluded from the sample. As a part of this discussion include how the inclusion or exclusion of the outliers may affect the larger sample.

As you analyze your research questions with inferential statistical techniques, it is not enough to report statistical significance. Increasingly, the practical significance in the way of effect sizes is expected. If your data demonstrate statistical significance without a large effect size, you will want to discuss that in chapter five. Actually, you will discuss both, regardless of whether they are consistent with each other or in contrast. For effect sizes, the traditional measures were defined by Cohen as .2 for a small effect, .5 medium, and .8 a large effect, but the Institute of Education Sciences suggests that for educational research an effect size as low as .25 may be "substantively important" (Cohen, 1992; What Works Clearinghouse, 2014). Cohen (1992) also provides advice on the sample size needed to achieve sufficient statistical power, so if you are conducting a mixed or quantitative study, his brief article[18] is a must-read.

---

[18] Cohen, J. (1992). A power primer. *Psychological bulletin, 112*(1), 155-159. http://www2.psych.ubc.ca/~schaller/528Readings/Cohen1992.pdf

Reporting statistical analyses can become tedious if you must report on the same techniques for multiple research questions or variables. Resist the temptation to merely copy and paste sections of your findings. Reading work that has been copied and pasted is dreadful. To make it more interesting for yourself, think about what the statistics are reporting and aim to include the real world language of what the statistical tests represent. This will not only offer you more ways to write about your analyses, but also it will prepare you to discuss your findings with your committee. Each of the symbols in a formula represents something, and familiarizing yourself with the actual formulas, rather than just the computer outputs, may facilitate your writing.

Above all you want to communicate your results clearly so that anyone, whether they have taken statistics or not, can understand what you found in your data. You may have used elegant math, but if the reader doesn't know what you found, it was not communicated effectively. Seek to find a balance between text, tables and figures so that the reader comes away with a clear picture of what you uncovered. They may not know what it means to your study yet (remember you are saving that for chapter five), but they know what you found.

Expectations for Qualitative Results

The expectations for reporting qualitative data are the same, whether your study is wholly qualitative or a mixed methods design. For a dissertation, you report on the qualitative analysis in chapter four, but include the full text of all the data as an appendix[19]. In order to include sufficient results in chapter four, you may want to use multiple forms of

---

[19] While the full data (transcripts or other documents) are included as appendices, remember to clean them for identifiers. You may have to redact (or black out) any names, addresses or other identifiers according to best practices and confidentiality requirements.

reporting. You might include a table of your themes and codes, or a graphic on how they relate, or you may have a summary table with your codes and definitions. Additionally, there may be tables of quotes addressing each research question, or frequency tables quantifying the qualitative data.

Most frequently, qualitative data are reported in the text of your document with quotes selected from the larger body of data. Just as with the quantitative data, context is important. Describe the participant providing the quote, not to identify him or her, but to allow the reader to better appreciate the quote. The subject description can pressure you into using pseudonyms. If you choose to do this, consider the implications previously discussed in chapter six.

Ultimately, your goal in reporting the qualitative findings is to help the reader understand the data you have collected; be sure to get a feel for the larger body of data. You include all the data as an appendix to demonstrate that you were faithful in your interpretation. Remember when analyzing qualitative data, your natural biases act as a filter. Your committee and any other reader of your work may have a different filter and so you want to ensure that they can see what you saw. This level of transparency, in conjunction with your discussion of your research philosophy, supports your credibility in drawing conclusions in the next chapter.

You can interpret qualitative findings with some quantitative techniques in addition to reporting some of the representative quotations and the themes you have found. Many qualitative analysis programs will perform counting functions on your data. You can ask these programs to count word frequencies, if you are investigating how participants talked about something, or code frequencies. Not every project or every researcher wants to include statistical procedures in qualitative work; some find that the quantification gets in the way of describing the experiences of the participants.

Depending on your inclination and your data, you can apply statistical techniques such as a chi-square analysis to determine if code frequencies differ between groups (i.e. Did urban and suburban report positive experiences with different frequency? You would determine the percentage of your sample that was urban vs. suburban and use that percentage to calculate the expected frequency based on the total number of positive codes. Then, you would calculate the chi-square statistic, and p-value[20].) Here is an abbreviated example of what this looks like with a sample that is 40% urban. I have eliminated some rows and columns of the table so that you could focus only on a couple of instances which demonstrate statistical significance.

Table 1.
Frequencies of References to Power Bases by Setting

	Expert	Legitimate
Urban	10 (6)*	35 (26.8)*
Suburban	5 (9)*	32 (40.2)*

Observed (expected)
*p < .05. **p < .01. ***p < .001.

When the frequencies are evaluated disaggregated by setting (Table 1), there is a significant difference in the observed and expected frequencies of references to the expert base of power, $\chi^2(1, N = 15) = 4.444, p = .035$. Urban educators referred to expert power more frequently than their suburban counterparts. Urban educators also referenced legitimate power more frequently, $\chi^2(1, N = 67) = 4.182, p = .040$.

---

[20] There are lots of programs that will help you do this, but if you want one that is free and online, try Preacher, K. J. (2001, April). Calculation for the chi-square test: An interactive calculation tool for chi-square tests of goodness of fit and independence [Computer software]. Available from http://quantpsy.org.

100

In the example above, the frequencies were generated by a query in NVivo 10.2.2 (version 11 is already available). When NVivo showed me that there were 15 passages that were coded as references to expert power and 67 instances of legitimate power codes, then I multiplied the total numbers by .4 and .6 to calculate the expected values. The expected values assume that the code frequency would be a function of the proportion of the sample. If the groups were similar, then the observed values would not differ from the expected values.

Quantitative analyses like these can also help focus what types of quotes are pulled for discussion. If I have groups that are dissimilar, then I would aim to illustrate that in my choices of representative quotes from my transcripts. Finding a lack of significant differences also guides decision-making and shapes discussion. When you are writing up your results, you want to be as true to the data as possible. You are describing what you have found without interpretation.

Moving Forward May Make You Go Back

It is possible that your analyses and findings may provide you with additional research questions and serendipitous findings. You may decide that after seeing the data, there was something else that is important to discuss. Like the overly narrow closet at the beginning of the chapter, when there are adjustments that need to be made, make them throughout the document.

If you see something in your data that bears further discussion in chapter five, add a section to chapter two to provide a foundation for interpretation. If, however, you see something in your data that is interesting, but there is not the literature to support any interpretation, do not report the findings with a newly added research question; rather, report them independently, and in chapter five you will only discuss them in the future research section.

You do want to keep that earlier map of variables and concepts handy, as your findings can bring you down a rabbit's hole of "what ifs?" Stay true to the focus of your research study. Remember you delimited your research for a reason. If your data answer your research questions and more, great! If your data answer your research questions and encourage you to write another dissertation as well, stop! Talk to your mentor. You may have found data that will make a nice article, but the analyses need to be excluded from your dissertation work. Your mentor can help you make those sorts of decisions.

Self-Assessment

This chapter will likely take a while to write, and frequently requires changes to the earlier chapters. Collecting your data and analyzing it requires dedication and skill. This self-assessment will help you determine whether you are ready to move on and use the notes and comments you have made while writing this chapter to write chapter five.

Criterion	Yes	Not Yet
Does your findings chapter include an initial description of how it is organized?	☐	☐
Is your finding chapter organized by your research question(s)?	☐	☐
Did you include direct references to your research questions and any relevant research hypotheses to clarify which findings are related to which questions and hypotheses?	☐	☐
Are you keeping a running record of interesting thoughts and interpretations of your findings to aid in your writing of the discussion in the next chapter?	☐	☐
Have you referred to every table you included within the text of the chapter?	☐	☐
Is every table necessary?	☐	☐
Have you ensured that data are not overly repeated in table and in the text?	☐	☐
Have you checked the APA (or other style guide as appropriate for your program) format of tables?	☐	☐

For quantitative studies, have you included effect sizes?	☐ ☐
For qualitative studies, have you included the raw data as appendices?	☐ ☐
For either quantitative, qualitative, or mixed methods studies, have your analyses been consistent with the best practices for your chosen procedure? Are you sure? Have you checked with the references you listed in your data analysis section?	☐ ☐
If you had additional findings beyond your initial research question(s), did you update the earlier parts of your dissertation?	☐ ☐
If you had additional findings beyond your initial research question(s), and there was no peer reviewed literature available to support discussion, did you make a note to include the discussion of these results only in the implications for future research section of chapter five and nowhere else?	☐ ☐
Does this chapter have an introduction, body and conclusion as do the rest of the chapters?	☐ ☐
Are you starting to build a list of your tables and figures that you will need when you are finished writing your document?	☐ ☐

Conclusion

How you present your findings will influence the ease with which you develop your discussion and draw your conclusions. While you want to include sufficient detail, it is tempting to present the same data in multiple formats to lengthen your document. You do not get a prize for the longest dissertation. Sadly, an overly long, repetitive section will actually hurt your credibility. It tells the reader that you don't know the best way to present your data.

You are earning your place in the academy, and the path to get there is through your original research. Immerse yourself in your data and let it make the argument for you. Follow it where it is leading you, rather than trying to force it in the direction you thought it was going. Recognize that you have bias, as does everyone else, and actively and transparently seek to mitigate the influence your bias may have on your data.

At this point in your project, your research home is really taking shape. You have installed the drywall and can tell how each room is going to look. Just because you can see what it will look like when you are done, you should not stop your quality control! A messy taping job will haunt you when you go to paint, so make sure that everything you do when working on your research home is done with care.

The nice part about writing your findings is that you are not collecting data anymore; you are pulling it together. You are reaping the rewards of your hard work. Take a bit of time to appreciate the work you have accomplished already. It is like plugging in a lamp and radio in your newly-wired outlet and ordering a pizza. Sure, you don't have dishes or furniture, but you have a house with electricity, plumbing, and walls!

Chapter 9: Drawing Conclusions and Defending

So you have chosen a site, developed plans, laid a foundation, framed, inspected, and dry-walled your house. Now you get to turn it into your home by choosing your last finishes, furnishings, and decorating it to make it yours. This is no trivial process; it can take a lot of time and energy to get it just right. Additionally, some people seem to have a knack for it, while others struggle. During this process it is important to alternate between paying close attention to detail and taking a big picture view.

Hopefully, you have been keeping a record of your thoughts on your data while you were writing your findings chapter. I am stressing this because personally, I failed to do so and spent a lot of time trying to remember what I had thought when I was first looking at my data. I remembered how it felt, and how excited I was, but not exactly what I had been excited about. That was very frustrating. It also changed my practice. Now when I look at data, I write down every idea, even if it may be far-fetched. (It is usually in some odd color highlighter on a scrap of paper, but I am working on finding a digital space that works for me to record these things.)

If you have a record of your inspired ideas, review it completely before you start to outline what you might write. This is also a perfect time to read your dissertation from start to finish. Don't fix things as you go; just add a comment or sticky note where something needs to be tweaked and keep reading. This re-read will help you cultivate a big picture view as you organize your discussion and conclusions.

Goals of this Chapter

Your final chapter intends to pull everything together, like a consistent decorative theme. Here is where you answer your research question(s). You are seeking to integrate your work in earlier chapters and your data. You are looking at your data and findings in light of the work of other researchers before you which you included in your earlier chapters and the relevant theory(ies). In this chapter you will explore the implications of your work, nailing the "so what?" question with detailed discussion of how your study is useful for better understanding the theory, investigating the concepts, guiding practice, and informing policy.

If you have chosen to earn a practitioner's doctorate, the Ed.D., the practical value of your work must be carefully delineated in this chapter. The researcher earning a Ph.D. does not have the same requirements; as a Ph.D. candidate there is an emphasis on creating new academic knowledge, rather than knowledge that can be applied in the field.

This chapter also provides the means to evaluate and discuss your research question(s). While it may have been challenging not to integrate the conclusions based on your data in chapter four, now you can explore these conclusions fully. In your first two chapters, you were analyzing, summarizing, and integrating the work of others; in chapter five, you find your voice. Your chapter five is where you pull it all together!

Writing the Chapter

If you have taken the time to re-read your document up to this point and your notes on your data, you are ready to outline chapter five. I am strongly recommending an outline, as researchers have a tendency to wander during this chapter, and this lack of focus undermines the hard work done to get to this point. Remember that this chapter, like the others, needs an introduction, a well-developed body with subheads, and a conclusion.

In developing your outline, be guided by your research question(s) and your previous writing. You will use the key citations in chapters one and two to support the interpretation of your data to answer your research question(s); therefore, you will have your research question(s) as a driving force for your organization, followed by the order or method your used to present your findings in chapter 4 and finally, by any patterns you used to organize your review of the literature (Figure 2). Together, these help structure how you discuss your findings.

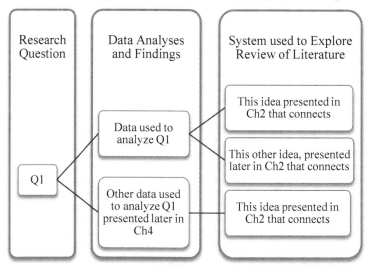

Figure 2. How the order of research questions, presentation of data, and organization of the review of literature influences the sequence of the discussion in chapter 5.

By maximizing the structures that are already present in your document, you remind the reader that you have thoughtfully planned and executed your research. This attention to detail will keep your writing grounded and reduce the likelihood that you will find yourself in a tangle of tangents that will be hard to connect. Here, as in the rest of your document, transitions between ideas are still required. Sure, your committee will read every page of your document, but there will be others (once it is publicly available) who will read your abstract and then, only your chapter five. Sad, but true. People want to know what they can learn from your research, and this is where you lay all of that out.

Once you have a plan for how you are going to lay out the sections of this chapter, treat each section as if it were its own research paper. Provide a brief introduction to the section, explaining how it will address a research question or an element of the research question, then develop the section fully. Draw upon your data, your notes on what you thought during your analyses, and the relevant references mentioned in chapters one and two.

Use each section to fully interpret your findings and support the claims you make with both your data and the published literature. Basically, if it was interesting enough to include in chapter four, then you will have a section or subsection dissecting the findings and evaluating the value of the findings. This is not to say that some of your data are unworthy, but what is the value of what you have found in the larger context of what has been previously published? Are your findings consistent with the existing body of literature, congruent with the theory, or are they anomalous? If you determine that your findings are inconsistent with prior research, offer possible explanations from what you know about your sample, or how the field has changed.

For each section, include the practical implications of your work. Perhaps a discussion of your findings leads you to a recommendation for practice. Develop that recommendation through your discussion section and ground it in your data. Be explicit as to how someone can use your work to improve theirs. A caution here… make sure any recommendations you make stem directly from your data. There may be temptation to allow bias into this section, conflating what you thought you knew before your data collection and what you actually found as a result of your study.

Finally, when you are ready to wrap up a section with its own conclusion, double check to make sure that you have actually answered the research question. I have read several drafts of chapter five where the doctoral candidate thought they had answered the research question, but they had left that very important piece in their head rather than include it in the document. Perhaps you may want to change the color of the text on where you answer the research question while you are writing so you can very clearly see where the answer has been included.

As you move from section to section, and from subsection to subsection, have conversations with yourself about what your results could mean. I don't mean to be schizophrenic, though in certain ways, I do. You are the expert in your topic and your data; nobody knows it as well as you do, so there is no other person that can play as effective a devil's advocate. Try to pick apart your discussion. Imagine your least-preferred coworker or classmate has presented that section or subsection to you, and look for any weaknesses in the way the argument was built or the quantity or quality of references. Don't try to fix flaws as you are tearing into your work; just note the area of weakness. You will do a better job of tearing it apart if you are not worried about how you will fix it later. Depending on your personality and writing habits, you may find it helpful to work on another section of your chapter five before you effect repairs on the one you just pulled apart.

Though it may seem counter-intuitive, this self-inflicted, brutal assault on your work will promote a better end product[21]. Take the time to reflect on each section as a

---

[21] Perhaps you remember how muscle tissue is built. Tiny micro-tears in the existing muscle tissue heal and strengthen. You may be sore two days after the workout, but you are stronger.

separate document, as you might appreciate a lovely room for the way the wall color, flooring, and furnishings all come together to create a feeling. Rarely is the first arrangement of furnishings the most appealing. Things get moved around and tested out, some things may get removed altogether in an effort to make the space perfect. You are creating such spaces in your dissertation.

As you begin to patch up the holes you tore in your work, look for any new resources that can update and enhance your review of the literature. You are coming close to the home stretch, so now is the best time to bolster any areas of weakness. You may also want to engage in some sort of unintentional plagiarism check. Some of the most popular tools can't be purchased by an individual, only an institution, but I googled plagiarism checker and got over three million hits. So, you can see if your institution has a good tool (or if a colleague or friend's does) or try a couple of the less prestigious ones.

Limitations and Delimitations

Once you have evaluated your research question(s) and any unanticipated findings with their own sections, you will launch into a new heading, one that will discuss the possible influence your limitations and delimitations have had on your research. Don't pull any punches here. You were limited by things beyond your control, but just because they were beyond your control does not mean that you don't have to evaluate how they may have impacted your data, as well as the conclusions that you based on those data. Be thorough and detailed.

I was going to say after this, address your delimitations, but it really doesn't matter which you explore first. I can see a fine approach with either leading into the other, just make sure you have a transition between the sections. (Have I stressed transitions enough?) With your delimitations you will need to be even more detailed, because you chose to delimit your study this way. You may have done

110

this to make the project manageable, but what does that mean for the person reading your study? They may not care that you have a job and a life; they want to know how conducting your research in your sample rather than studying everyone in the population may be affecting the results. Don't get defensive; just explain how the results and conclusions are impacted.

The limitations and even more so the delimitations are the seeds from which your recommendations for future research will grow. For every limitation you mention, there is a way to study that does not have that limitation. If you used a quantitative approach to study your variables, then you are limited by the statistical procedures. A qualitative approach does not have that limitation, so therefore, you may wish to suggest that your study be repeated utilizing qualitative means.

Each of your delimitations will also have a corresponding paragraph or so in the recommendations for a future research section. If you delimited your setting, as you probably did, then you will recommend it be replicated in other settings. The key here is which other settings, and why? You will read the generic sentence calling for replication in other settings, but a high-quality dissertation will tell the reader more.

You may have also included some recommendations for practice in the earlier sections in this chapter. Each of those is another opportunity for a recommendation for future research. Look back through the sections and consider how each of your recommendations could be evaluated and describe those here.

Wrapping up Chapter Five

This is so exciting! You are now in the final sections of your last chapter. Okay, you will have a couple more sections before your last section—the conclusion. These last sections, with their own headings, discuss the implications for research (in general) and the implications for your chosen field (mine was Educational Leadership but for my students, they address both Educational Leadership and Policy because their degree will be in Educational Leadership and Policy Studies).

The general implications for research section centers on what you have learned about research by conducting your study. This is essentially about what you found about your methodology within your setting; perhaps there was a glitch that someone else could avoid if he/she were conducting a study in a similar study, or big picture ideas that came out of your limitations and delimitations. This section is your way to "pay it forward" to any other researcher (including future doctoral students) who reads your dissertation.

Your field-specific section of implications takes your discussion a bit further, requiring you to generalize what you found in the individual sections implications pieces into a larger (not longer) synthesis. Consider how your research advances your field. How can other researchers (and practitioners) capitalize on your work to prepare for new or continuing projects that relate to your field?

Here we are, at the last section of the last chapter. Your conclusion is an opportunity to present the key elements of the knowledge resulting from your dissertation and possible future work on your dissertation topic. This is a brief section, just a few paragraphs to synthesize the results and discussion of your research and a paragraph or two that highlights the implications of the study in view of the social significance of the research.

Your conclusion serves as the high-impact piece you include in a room to give it style, the "wow factor". Using the room analogy, it might be a bold textile choice, an eye-catching painting or area rug; in your dissertation, it is the conclusion section of chapter five. You don't want to overstate your findings, but you want the results of your research to make an impression.

After the Draft

I am not talking about the NFL draft, but something possibly even more important: the completed draft of your dissertation. It is not quite ready for your committee. You need to craft an abstract to summarize your work. This is not a time to copy and paste. You may be tired, but don't skimp on this. If you need to, take a couple days off, and then grab your tablet or phone and record the answer to these questions in order, out loud. What was the problem you studied? How did you study it? What did you find?

When you type up your verbal response, hope that it is near the word limit for your abstract. A rough estimate is that natural speech is about 130 words per minute. Each program is going to have its own word limits for an abstract. They generally range anywhere from a skimpy 100 words up to a generous 350 words. My program has a 150-word limit. Your abstract is the first introduction to your work that anyone gets and indeed, could be all they ever see of it, so it behooves you to craft your abstract carefully.

In addition to your abstract, there may be other front pages you have to generate, like your table of contents (I provided some samples on pages 1-6 of this text) as well as lists of tables and figures that include the exact labels of the tables and figures. Here is where I *do* recommend you copy and paste. The easiest way I have found to create these tables is to use a two-column table, with a large column for the text and a skinny one for the page numbers. Once you have everything entered into the table, format the table without gridlines, and *poof!*, you have beautifully formatted page. I wish I had figured that out back when I was writing my own dissertation. I tried to use the table of contents feature in MSWord, but no matter what it tells you, MSWord does not really know APA formatting.

Another element of your dissertation that seems extra are the appendices. Each appendix is labeled (A-Z) and includes a descriptive title. The appendices must be labeled (A, B, C...) in the order in which they appear in the dissertation text. So, if you need to include an appendix[22] and you didn't reference it, go back into the text and figure out where it belongs.

The last element of the document is your list of references. Depending on how vigilant you have been along the way, this can either be a breeze or a tantrum inducing pain in the @$$. I wish I had been using a reference managing program for my dissertation as I am doing for this manuscript. Actually, I am not sure they existed at that point. In any event, if you are using a program like that, and you cleaned the data in the program itself, then it is just a matter of double-checking.

If you are working on your dissertation the way I was working on mine, your references section is a jumble of properly-formatted citations, notes, and random URLs. I am sorry, and I feel your pain. Each reference in the list needs to be properly formatted, and wherever possible, a digital object identifier (doi) included. For me, the annoying part was ensuring I had a 1:1 ratio of sources. Only materials that you actually referenced can show up in your reference list, so if you edited out a sentence with a citation but forgot to delete it from your reference list, you don't have a 1:1 ratio.

Again, if you are using a citation managing program, this is automatic, but if not, grab a friend and a highlighter. Print out your work and have him/her read every parenthetical citation out loud to you and you highlight them when you have found them in your reference list. If they are not there, circle

---

[22] One example of this is your IRB approval letter. When you wrote chapter three you may not have had IRB approval, so you wouldn't have a reference to the appendix, but it is a required appendix, so chapter three has to be edited to include a reference to it. By the way, you don't have to say "see" when referring to the appendix, you can just parenthetically list the appendix, e.g. (Appendix C) if it is the third appendix listed in the document.

114

them in the document for you to investigate later. This is very time-consuming, so you may want to use five different friends, or trade help with other people in your doctoral program.

Once your document is nearly complete, engage an editor. I mentioned that I asked a math teacher colleague to read mine; depending on your needs, you may want a professional. The perks of hiring someone is that you can be more demanding. If you are asking someone to edit your work as a favor, you can't be very pushy on the timeline or the level of detail. If you employ an editor, be clear on your expectations. Do you expect them to fix errors they see or just note them?

Sharing the Draft

Now, you know how long and hard you have worked on this, and your committee is partially aware of that. It is going to take them some time to read this document and provide feedback. Two to three weeks is reasonable. While you are waiting for feedback, you can be planning your dissertation defense presentation or plan your post-defense life. You can also prepare yourself for the very frustrating rounds of revisions.

When you think that your document is nearly complete, it is very hard to hear that changes are requested, particularly when you believe the person has already seen that section and didn't say it needed edits. Remember, you picked your committee because you know they want what is best for you and will help you create the strongest product. Of course you want your work to be awesome, but getting there can be an emotional roller coaster.

Just today, I had a reminder of what this feels like. I have been working on a grant proposal and the office reviewing the grant and I have been through several drafts. Yesterday, I received an email saying, "This looks great. All I did was insert one missing space between two words on the third page... this can be the project narrative we'll send out." Today, I received another emails from the same person, "After reading through the program narrative's guidelines one more time – there were a few more questions...." These were not small questions, but rather significant questions that required rewriting sections of the proposal. I admit, I was frosted (very annoyed), but then considered that the person was thinking about my work, and wanted to position me to be successful in winning the grant. I had to get out of my own way to appreciate that receiving the further edits was better, in terms of my proposal, than getting the email saying it was all set.

Remember the advice in earlier chapters; provide specific guidance on areas on which you would like your readers and mentor to focus. You may experience slightly longer wait times, as your committee is making sure that your document is good enough for them to sign as a high-quality product. Forever, your committee's signatures are attached to your work; they certify that it is of sufficient quality and that is not something taken lightly. At earlier stages it was about whether your work was good enough for you to keep moving forward; now, it is about their professional reputations, hence, there is an increased level of scrutiny just before you defend your dissertation.

Once you have your mentor's approval, it is time to schedule the dissertation defense. Again, this is a public performance of your work, but your audience may be different. You may wish to include some of the people who have helped you reach this point. It is less important that you have the best professional minds around the table, because your research has already been completed. There is not a lot you can do with the feedback from the audience at this point. Take a deep breath and try to coordinate three busy schedules and your own.

When you have determined the date for your defense, make sure that your committee has a best possible (I hope it is done!) version of your dissertation. Since you only need three,

116

consider a nice binding.[23] The binding, or lack thereof, will not influence your success; it is the quality of your work that merits a degree.   Still, there is some tangible boost in confidence that comes with delivering a bound product that could serve you well.   Make sure your committee has this version, that includes your university's required front pages at least three weeks before your defense date.[24]

You have already been through this process at your proposal hearing. The dissertation defense is similar. You want to make sure that everyone who attends will have an understanding of your research, even if they have not read your whole dissertation. There will likely be only four people in the room who have read your whole document: you and your committee. Consider the handouts you made for your proposal hearing. Did anyone provide you with feedback on them at the proposal stage? This is your chance to use that feedback.

You want to make sure that everyone has access to the key information in your 20-minute presentation. You don't get more time, even though you have more to say! This means you can't just add to what you did for the proposal. You might keep a few graphics, but most of the presentation centers on the findings, conclusions, and implications of your research. A rule of thumb is that roughly 25% of your presentation is on chapters 1-3 and 75% focuses on chapters 4 and 5.

Double-check with your mentor before you decide to use a novel approach to presenting your work. Most committees expect a PowerPoint-style presentation with a reliance on your research questions, brief bullets, tables, and graphics. With the exception of qualitative dissertations that

---

[23] This website and others offer fancy softcover binding for about $20 a copy. http://phdbookbinding.com/thesis-and-dissertation-book-printing-and-binding/ I priced a version that included the university seal ($21) and one without ($17).

[24] Three weeks is a good rule of thumb; please check your program's guidelines for any program-specific requirements.

may display some key quotes, there is insufficient time to have multiple text-heavy slides.

You are welcoming the public to see what you have accomplished, and you control how that is received. How have you organized your handouts? What have you chosen to include as handouts? Consider your proposal hearing as a guide. Did you have too many handouts, or was the text so small that people didn't seem to be looking at them? At a minimum have your presentation slides, models, research questions, instruments, tables and illustrations available for your audience to review. If you conducted a qualitative study, you are encouraged to include a table of quotes, themes, and code memos/definitions for your audience.

It will be difficult to summarize your work in twenty minutes, but this is what academics do all the time when they present at conferences, so the audience at the university is aware of your constraints. Practice what you are going to say, and time yourself. You only have about 5 minutes for chapters 1-3, so you will have to make difficult choices. Most of your literature review will not be a part of your presentation. When you are confident that your handouts are ready and you can present your work in twenty minutes, ask your mentor if they want to hold a dry run a week or so before the actual defense. If you are ready, this can be a great way to make adjustments to your presentation while giving you time to practice the adjusted presentation.

On the day of your defense you will invariably be nervous. This is totally normal and totally unproductive. Do what you can to be extra prepared. Since your audience will have handouts, if the worst case scenario happens and the projector bulb blows at the start of your presentation, don't worry; they can just follow along on paper. People presented dissertations before there were computers and digital projectors. Try not to get flustered, and know that there is nobody else that knows more about your research than you do.

After you finish your presentation there will be a bit of time for questions and answers. It is unlikely that someone will ask you a question that you are unable to answer. If you get a question you haven't considered, you can say that. Most of the questions from audience members will be about what, if anything, was surprising? What would you change if you were doing this again? How will you share your findings to a wider audience? These open ended questions are a sign of appreciation for your hard work and are giving you a platform to reflect on the process.

You might get a question about whether you had considered author X or model Y for your study. If you have, then politely answer honestly. If you have not, then say who you did read and describe why the model you chose was most appropriate. Answer with confidence. This is not the day to doubt yourself.

Once the committee and audience have asked questions and you have succinctly yet brilliantly answered them, the committee will torture you by making you and the rest of the audience leave the room while they decide your fate. Have a plan for where you and your guests, if you brought some, will go. You don't want to be a group of people milling in the hall. Perhaps one of your committee members will let you sit in his/her office, or maybe there is a room with sufficient chairs for you to wait comfortably. While you are waiting, your committee is deciding what changes must be made to your document before it is ready for publication.

Rarely is there a document that doesn't need any edits at all after the defense. The most likely scenario is that your committee will agree that you have passed your defense and there are revisions (either major or more hopefully minor) that must be completed before you get the signature page. Your committee will invite you, not your guests, back into the room and tell you how you did. Assuming you passed, YEA!, you will set a due date for the revisions.

Now you can go out to celebrate your success! Congratulations. Wait, the book isn't done? I owe you one more self-assessment.

Self-Assessment

Since this is the last self-assessment, and arguably the most important, it is a little longer. In particular, a large portion of this self-assessment is dedicated to appendices, as that seems to be an area of concern when documents come to the committee. While I have tried to put everything I can in this list, as you near your program's completion, pay extra special attention to the program's guidelines and the universities requirements.

Criterion	Yes	Not Yet
Have you completed the universities requirements for graduation with the exception of your dissertation defense?	☐	☐
Have you used the program and university guidelines to format your document?	☐	☐
Throughout your document, are the research question(s) worded exactly the same way?	☐	☐
Have you checked for other inconsistencies?	☐	☐
Have you scoured your document and made sure that it is in the past tense where appropriate?	☐	☐
Have you clearly answered your research question(s)?	☐	☐
If you had colored the text that answered your research question(s) a different color, have you make it all black?	☐	☐
Does chapter five provide a full discussion of all the findings that integrates references from earlier in the document?	☐	☐
Does chapter five go beyond the interpretations aligned with chapter two and provide additional alternate explanations based on insights gleaned from the experience of researching the problem?	☐	☐
Is the discussion grounded in evidence?	☐	☐
Is it true that no new data has been introduced in chapter five?	☐	☐

120

Is there a discussion of the implications of the limitations? ☐ ☐

Is there a discussion of the implications of the delimitations? ☐ ☐

Has the impact of the chosen setting(s) been discussed? ☐ ☐

Have additional findings that do not have a peer-reviewed research base, limitations, delimitations, and any recommendations for practice made earlier in the chapter all been used to suggest future research opportunities? ☐ ☐

Is there a significant discussion of how this research advances theory or practice? ☐ ☐

Is there a thoughtfully crafted discussion of the implications for research presented? ☐ ☐

Did you present implications for your field (whatever the name is on your doctoral degree)? ☐ ☐

Does your conclusion synthesize your project as a whole? ☐ ☐

Does your conclusion include the larger social significance of your research? ☐ ☐

Have you outlined where you feel this research ought to be advanced in the near future in your conclusion? ☐ ☐

Are all your references in the approved style (APA, etc.)? ☐ ☐

Do you have a strict 1:1 ratio of references? ☐ ☐

Are your references in alphabetical order? ☐ ☐

Are all your appendices labeled with titles and a designated letter? ☐ ☐

Are the appendices labeled and included in the order in which they are referenced in the text? (Note: if it is referenced more than once, it only has the label of the first time it appears in the document. It can't be Appendix A and F, it would only be Appendix A.) ☐ ☐

Is every appendix referenced in the text? ☐ ☐

Have you included all the following as appendices if you have used them?: ☐ ☐

A blank copy of any instrument ☐ ☐

A blank copy of consent documents ☐ ☐

A blank copy of any demographic data collection form(s) ☐ ☐

Scripts or protocols for instructions or interviews ☐ ☐

Any instructions used by researcher or participant(s)	☐	☐
Permission letters from data collection sites	☐	☐
Permission letters for any copyrighted measures	☐	☐
Observer or Rater trainings, instructions, and forms	☐	☐
Any advertisements for participant solicitation	☐	☐
Any communication, digital or hard copy connected with securing participation, reminding participants, or encouraging completion.	☐	☐
NIH certificate	☐	☐
IRB Approval letter	☐	☐
Raw data that were analyzed for a qualitative dissertation	☐	☐
Code memo book	☐	☐
Have you planned for some time after the dissertation hearing to make the likely revisions?	☐	☐
Is your presentation is 20-minutes in duration?	☐	☐
Does your presentation focus on chapters 4 & 5 (75%)?	☐	☐
Do your handouts include every table and graphic that an audience member might want to inspect?	☐	☐
Have you provided your audience with copies of your presentation slides?	☐	☐
Have you included relevant text such as your title, problem statement, theoretical framework, and research questions on audience handouts in a very readable font?	☐	☐
Have you provided the audience with the relevant findings (either qualitative or quantitative) so they can look at your quotes, themes, and codes or numerical data including levels of significance and effect sizes?	☐	☐
Have you decided how you will celebrate?	☐	☐

Conclusion

Your conclusion chapter to your dissertation does more than complete the document; it pulls all your work together. When you established the problem in chapter one, that was great, but it didn't offer any benefit to the reader. Your review of the literature was crafted with care, skillfully exploring what was already known about your variables into an argument, but that was just preparing the reader for what was to come. You carefully explained what you did and what you found, but those chapters didn't have a context. Your conclusion is where your data become meaningful. It is where the argument you shaped in chapter two truly comes to life. Your conclusion is where you establish yourself as a member of the academy.

How you have crafted your concluding chapter expresses, to some extent, who you are as an academic. The choices you have made up to this point in your dissertation are displayed in this final chapter. To apply our home building analogy: you know those television shows where different individuals or teams are given similar or even identical homes or rooms to decorate, and at the show's end, the spaces are entirely different from each other? A dissertation is similar. You and another candidate could have the exact same data and results, but the conclusions you draw and the implication you see will vary, based on your past experiences and your research philosophies.

Your dissertation defense, too, will differ from any other researcher's, because you too, are different. Some elements of your defense will be similar as they are required by your program, but how you share your research is a function of who you are. This is your housewarming party where you invite people to see what you have constructed. I remember being incredibly proud of my work at my housewarming party, but also knowing that there were more projects I wanted to tackle. It's the same in research. Even as you are presenting what you have accomplished, you will make recommendations for what comes next. And, just as there are cups and plates to clean up after a party, your committee will likely have things that need to be cleaned up in your document, but in the end, your research home, like your dissertation, will be even nicer when it is clean.

Chapter 10: Now What?

Hello, Doctor! Once you have successfully defended your dissertation and cleaned up any remaining edits, your committee will sign off on your work, thereby admitting you to the academy. Welcome! What is weird is that you can't predict how you will feel about begin called "Doctor". For me, it was a bit uncomfortable. I didn't feel smarter or more qualified, so I felt a bit like an imposter. It turns out that this is a perfectly normal way to feel (Laursen, 2008; Parkman, 2016), though I didn't know that at the time.

I also felt a bit lost. For the past years I had a goal toward which I was constantly working. If I was relaxing, I defined it as taking a break from working on my dissertation. But now that I finished, I was just done. I had nothing to define my time. My work was rewarding, but not overly challenging, and what had been a challenge was now complete. I was anxious and sad but couldn't explain why to anyone, because I thought it sounded stupid that I wasn't happy that I had achieved my goal. As it turns out, feeling this way is not unique to me (Billups, 2016).

I am telling you this because I want you to know that however you feel when you have finished your dissertation is the way *you* are supposed to feel. Please don't beat yourself up because you experience this time in your life differently than some of your cohorts. I hope you are happy and satisfied with your work and gracefully move into the next phase of you life; even if it is bumpier than that initially, trust me, it does smooth out. I still prefer people call me Jess to Dr. Gregory (except the cable company; the customer service professionals can call me doctor instead of ma'am), but if I hear "Dr. Gregory", I still look to see if they are talking to me.

Curb Appeal

O.K., enough about me. Let's get back to what is next for *you*. Once you have your signatures on your dissertation, you will be able to navigate any university procedures for getting your degree posted. These vary by university, but usually involve making sure that the appropriate forms are signed by the right people and dropped off at the right offices. You may need to have a clean copy of your dissertation with these forms, or more and more frequently, a digital version.

Your university will have procedures set up for how it expects you to proceed towards the publication of your dissertation. That's right! Your dissertation will be available for other people to read all over the world. That is why you produced original research, right? To make an impact. Admittedly, while a published dissertation does have some impact, it is not as effective as other forms of publication.

Sharing your work with a larger audience is like dressing up the outside of your home. Whether you have a large acreage, a postage stamp lot, or just a doormat in a hallway, you encourage others to consider visiting your home in the way you present yourself to the outside world. How you disseminate your work is how you increase the curb appeal of your research home.

The most highly regarded means of disseminating information in my field is the peer-reviewed journal. I'm not going to mislead you; pulling together an article for publication is an art form in itself, but you have a lot of the work done already. A large part of the challenge in publishing in a journal lies in finding the right journal. You may have written a plum of an article, but if you send it to a journal that is a poor fit, it

126

will be rejected. Basically, you are looking to make sure that your research home fits in with the neighborhood. While in Bermuda it is encouraged, or even assumed, that you will paint your house a sunny pastel color, but that is not the case in every neighborhood. In some historical districts in New England there are restrictions on what color you paint your house. You need to investigate the expectations of the neighborhood before you finalize your manuscript.

Some journals have greater impact than others; some are very exclusive. Scimago[25] ranks journals and allows you to search by field. This listing, which you can sort by region or country, allows you to target journals that have sufficient reach for your work. Once you identify a journal or some journals, research the journal's aims and scope page. This information tells you what they look to publish. If your topic or methodology doesn't fit, move on and choose a different journal.

Your mentor can generally help you tease apart your larger dissertation into smaller, more focused topics for a journal article. You will likely not be able to copy and paste your way to a well-written journal article, because the writing styles of dissertations and journal articles differ. Whichever journal you choose, read many of the articles published in that journal and use them as models for style. You will also want to look to your intended journal for references. If your intended journal has not published any articles that are of interest to you, then ask yourself: why is this your intended journal?

If you are working with your mentor on an article that is coming from your dissertation research, you retain first authorship. The American Psychological Association (APA) is very clear on this point, authorship on a manuscript is ordered by the level of contribution. Perhaps one of your other committee members was more influential in shaping your

---

[25] http://www.scimagojr.com/journalrank.php?country=US

work; in that case, you would offer them second author. Now, what if you finished your dissertation *a while ago* and are just now breathing new life into it? You have to refresh the literature review and basically retool everything, but you are doing that without the benefit of your dissertation committee. Since you are essentially writing from scratch and the committee isn't making a big contribution to this work, inviting them to be listed as authors is collegial, but not obligatory.

Single author manuscripts tell the reader that you worked on this alone. They are great for establishing your expertise on a subject. Multiple author manuscripts don't indicate who did what or how influential they are, only that the first author did the lion's share of the work. It can be helpful to have an established author on a publication to increase its visibility. If I were writing on student retention and had the opportunity to get feedback from Vincent Tinto, I would certainly ask him to be a co-author. Basically, having him listed as a co-author, even if he only had time to review what I had written and provide feedback, would be substantive for my manuscript because of his reputation. You will have to make that call as you are developing your manuscript.

One other thing about peer-reviewed journals is that they are generally slow. Most of the individuals editing and reviewing for these academic journals are professors who do this as a service to the field. They have their regular full-time job with their own students and research. A fast journal gets back to you in a few weeks, but it is totally normal for 6 months to go by between submitting a paper and the journal getting back to you. Actually, once you get a little experience, you will hope it takes slightly longer because when a managing editor emails you right back, it is typically because they are rejecting your work. Note: they are not rejecting you, but your work doesn't fit with their aims and scope or perhaps it needs a deeper edit. Feel free to ask the editor why it was sent back if they don't volunteer it initially.

Let's assume your manuscript made it through the initial screening. Now, it goes out for peer review. This means it literally is sent to people to read and evaluate. So, unless your submission is awesome or awful, you will get a variety of comments from the reviewers. On the same manuscript, I received the following two comments: "The authors should be complimented for both the readability of the article (clear, articulate arguments made) and for the very strong review of literature provided. The literature review provided both context and justification for the study," Reviewer 1. "Generally, the manuscript is lengthy and includes a long introduction which is not necessary. Much information can be shorten, in my opinion. However, a deeper introduction on attitudes (state of art) is needed and should be add," Reviewer 2. It is important to not dismiss Reviewer 2's comments, because English does not appear to be his or her native language.

Any article you send out for peer review may come back with comments that are tough to read. The comments from Reviewer 1 look very positive, but the reviewer still recommended a major revision to the paper. When you look at the comments and then see the recommendation, it can be difficult to reconcile them. Reviewer 2 actually provided me more help with his or her comments, as I could use them to retool the article. Once you have made the revisions and resubmitted the manuscript, you wait again. This cycle can repeat with major and minor revisions. Each step of the process brings you a bit closer to publication, or so you think, though at any stage in the revision process the editor can send you a note that says "I regret to inform you that our reviewers have now considered your paper but unfortunately feel it unsuitable for publication." Ouch. It's painful, it's not fun, but it happens. Lick your wounds for a day or so, find another journal, and retool the manuscript so that it is even better than it was before.

Building Up

Perhaps you aren't sure you are ready to jump into writing a peer-reviewed article yet. Maybe you don't have the time, or (and I hope this is the case) you are reading this part of the book before you have finished your research. Another way to disseminate your research is through conference presentations and proceedings. Just as there is a range of peer-review journals, there is a range of conferences. Some are small and encourage participation from graduate students, and others are much larger. Consult with your mentor as to which might be most appropriate for your research and your career path.

Picking a target conference is not your only decision to make. Each conference will offer a variety of sessions, and you will need to choose which is most appropriate for your work. At the start of a project, before you have all your data, you may want to participate in a roundtable style session where you tell the other people at your table what you are thinking about doing and ask them for input. Once you are done with your research, many of the other formats are more appropriate.

The paper session is the traditional format to present work that has been completed. For this type of presentation, you must send a completed paper in advance of the presentation. Some conferences have conference proceedings in which your paper will be published. While this is a peer-reviewed publication, it is not considered the same as a peer-reviewed journal article. Please, carefully consider whether you want your paper included in the conference proceedings. If you do not intend to pursue journal publication of your work, then steam ahead. If you aren't sure, or you know that you will seek a journal publication for this data, then you may not want to include your work in the proceedings. Once your data are published in the proceedings, they are published. You can't double-dip unless you have a totally different article.

130

Like the peer-reviewed journal article, conference submissions go through peer-review. You can actually volunteer to serve as a proposal reviewer for a conference you are considering to see what the proposals look like, but if you do this, you have to care enough about it to offer the author of the proposal substantive feedback to improve his/her work. Unlike the nebulous timeline of a journal, conferences tend to run on very tight schedules. The organizers and reviewers are still volunteers with full-time jobs, but the nature of a conference requires that each step be completed in a timely manner. Look for the timetable on the conference website.

One last word about conferences. (I am on the Board of Directors for a couple organizations that hold conferences, so I can tell you this as an insider.) If you are accepted to present, actually go and present. There are some academics who submit proposals to conferences they do not intend to attend. This is an uncolleagial practice. Each conference is limited in time and space, and by accepting a space, someone else does not get a space. Additionally, the time and energy that reviewers spent reading and providing comments to improve the presentation at the conference does not aid the conference at all. Unfortunately, less scrupulous academics will continue this practice as they can list that the proposal was accepted for presentation on their CVs, but it taints the academic's reputation within the larger circle of researchers who perhaps went to a session to hear the presentation and had their time wasted due to a no-show.

Another key element to increasing your curb appeal is your relationships with your neighbors. When you attend a conference, you are among those who have similar research interests. Listen to them and share your thoughts; in short, be a good neighbor. Maybe you have had the experience of the neighbor who plays music too loud; this is analogous to the conference attendee who shows up to present and leaves directly afterwards. This is the type of person who is not considerate of anyone else. Being a good academic neighbor includes offering constructive questions and resources. A good neighbor may also simply listen well. When people meet a good academic neighbor at a conference, they tend to be more interested in staying connected.

It can be intimidating to attend a conference on your own; it necessitates you either be a good neighbor or be alone. I recommend the former. Early in the conference, strike up a conversation with a presenter whose work interests you. Gently pepper them with questions about their research and build an understanding of where your interests overlap. Perhaps this individual is at the conference with other colleagues. As you are introduced, you have now associated that entire group. Depending on your personality type, having one small group of people you recognize may be more than enough. If you are more naturally outgoing, advice on interacting with others is wasted here. You know what to do!

The first conference I attended on my own was the New England Educational Research Organization conference. I was anxious, but excited. The first day was pretty lonely. I attended a lot of sessions, but struggled at meals to choose where to sit. On the afternoon of the second day, I met a friendly soul who introduced me to a large contingent of faculty and doctoral students from her university. They were so nice! Being slightly awkward, I declined her dinner invitation (which was foolish) but agreed to come to the party they were having later. It turns out that this was the first party I had ever been to where they spontaneously started to pick up musical instruments and jam as a group. Seriously! I thought that only happened in TV shows and movies. People were laughing and singing while others played musical instruments. The point is, I would not have had that awesome experience if I wasn't willing to attend the conference alone. I learned a lot about being a good academic neighbor from the kindness that was extended to me.

Conclusion

The goal was to earn your doctorate and build your research home, but a part of the process is sharing your work so that others can learn from it. A way to draw people to your work is to make it available through publication and presentation. Even with a promise of candy on Halloween, people don't want to approach a house with no curb appeal. When it comes to developing the curb appeal for your research home, you have to make it easy to find.

You also have joined the academy as a function of earning your doctorate. You have privileges that you can exercise due to your status, like being called "doctor". You also have responsibilities as a colleague. If you want to serve as a journal or conference proposal reviewer, then you have to provide substantive, constructive feedback, and if you propose to present, then you present. In short, be a good academic neighbor.

Chapter 11: How Frequently Do Questions Need to be Asked?

I will be honest, I have only recently started reading FAQs. Before, I had a pretty unrealistic view that nobody else could have already entertained my questions. Turns out my questions were sometimes covered in the FAQ. I wanted to include a FAQ section in this text, but then it occurred to me that individuals seeking their doctorate may not frequently ask me the same questions. If a question is a good question, how many times does it have to be asked to be a good question? I am willing to say one time. So, in this section I have included questions that have been asked at least once.

I organized them to parallel the order of this text, and then provide a catch-all at the end. You will see that some of the ideas that were included in this document originated from questions (or statements) that my current and former students have asked.

Questions about the Big Picture

Q. Where can I get a broad overview of the parts of a dissertation?

Including this question was a little self-serving, but this question prompted my original monograph (2009) and this deeper treatment of the topic. Chapter one of this text offers an overview of the parts of a traditional dissertation.

Q. How should I go about choosing an appropriate committee for my dissertation?

Ok, another driving question for the text, but let me give the short answer here, and if you want more, you can go back into the text (Chapter 3). First by personality, second by expertise. Weird, right? You need to trust this person to guide you, which means you have to want to listen to them. If they are a super expert but you don't like them, it will not be as rewarding an experience for you.

Q. What would be an appropriate timeline in order to complete the dissertation within two years?

So, for everyone it is a little different. It depends on the competing demands on your time, the type of data you are collecting and the ease with which you can access that data. A rule of thumb is that in the first semester after comps (let's say it is a fall semester) you play around with a bunch of ideas that are connected to a general topic while you build the skills to create your proposal and conduct your research.

At the end of that semester, Dec/Jan, you work with your sponsor to begin really crafting the proposal. This can take as little as one semester, meaning that you defend your proposal at the end of the spring. Some people need the summer to get the proposal in shape, and others extend into fall. Keep in mind that you have to arrange schedules to hold the proposal hearing.

Don't dawdle too much in the proposal phase, or you won't make your targeted goal of completing your dissertation at the end of the second year. Also, each draft of a proposal, chapter, dissertation can take up to three weeks to read and get your feedback returned, so be judicious about submitting drafts. You want to polish work before sharing with the committee so you get the best, most specific feedback possible. Very "rough" drafts actually slow the process down a LOT!

Q. Would you be available to meet to go over the more substantive changes before I put things together?

When I was looking through my old emails to pull questions, this was the most frequently asked question of all. This request translates to, "will you help me think this through, I am insecure." I appreciate that a doctoral candidate doesn't want to spend time going in a direction that may not ultimately pay dividends, but there is something to be learned from thinking it through first and making the changes that make sense to you because after all, this is *your* dissertation.

Now, you have read that, and I have written it, and I still set up a time to meet with the student. I am not sure the student(s) got what he or she wanted, but we met. Generally, they came to my office and I had them answer all the questions that they posed to me. Sure, I was there with them, but they could have done this from their desk/couch/bed and not had to deal with parking on campus. The meeting probably slowed their progress; I didn't stop them from going down a dead end, but I walked alongside. When we got to the dead end, we exchanged looks across my desk and it was then that each of my students recognized that they were the guides.. I am fully okay with going down a lot of dead ends.

I would love to say that the experience of going down the dead end and my choice to refrain from rescuing us changed the behavior of those asking to meet to "go over" work. Based on my review of my email, that just isn't true. There must be another aspect of it (maybe this is an avenue for future research); perhaps a there is social side to it, and the act of meeting is a comfort. Either way, the request for time to meet is by far the greatest request.

If you are asking a professor to meet, whether they are on your committee or not, try to be considerate. Before I was in the job, I had no idea how many other demands there were on a professor's time. If you are aiming for a check-in, then check in and move on. If it is more substantive, and you want to work near your faculty member, be explicit. Some people will welcome you to share the work space and you can both be working at the same time; others will not be able to be productive with you there, and then you have essentially asked for a very large chunk of time.

Q. I am working my rear off on this, I am mentally and physically exhausted. Must sleep.

I know this isn't a question, but something I have seen over and over. When you are on a roll you just keep going until you get burnt out. It is very important to set limits. I am a binge writer, but every 25 minutes I have to acknowledge that this is a good time for a break and move a little. I appreciate that I have a pomodoro timer monitoring that for me, because I am not good at protecting myself.

While you are working towards your doctorate it can be tempting to work so hard that you let your health go. Bad plan. Use little breaks to go for a walk. You don't need stress and the sedentary aspect of this work to put your health in jeopardy. There is no badge for the least amount of sleep or the most weight gained. These are not competitions that you want to win.

Perhaps this seems counter-intuitive, but this is a wonderful time to develop a new healthy habit. Maybe you always wanted to practice meditation and mindfulness? Use your dissertation as an excuse. You want to focus on healthy eating, there are few better reasons than you find yourself sitting more than you would. Basically, require yourself to have balance.

Q. Is it wrong to copy and paste relevant parts of the dissertation?

For the most part, yes. The exceptions are your research question(s), any hypotheses, and your problem statement sentence. These really can't change across the dissertation, so feel free to copy and paste. Everything else, even if it seems repetitive, ought to be reworded to be slightly different.

Q. One person on my committee criticizes the limitations, another says its very well done! How do you please both people on that?

Take a deep breath, you do have to please your committee because they sign off on the quality of your work, but you do have a voice. What I read in that email was a lot of frustration, and a hope that I would tell him/her that no changes are required. I also saw that one person gave substantive feedback, and the other, general.

I was pretty sure that the critic had offered more useful feedback, but I suggested that the student ask both of them (starting with the critic), separately and non-confrontationally, what areas specifically could I improve? And for the committee member that generally praised the work: it was suggested that I modify X this way, would that detract from my work in your opinion or strengthen it?

Q. What do I do, I think Dr. Committee Member read the wrong version!?

I love this question. The student kept sending revision after revision, and while there were always minor differences, sometimes there were major ones, it was hard to keep the versions straight. This student was so motivated and eager to please, it was difficult to tell him/her that he/she had created the situation. This worked out fine, as it wasn't the final draft (far from it) of either the proposal or full dissertation.

To avoid this situation, be judicious and purposeful when sending drafts. With your mentor's counsel, send only polished drafts to committee members. Double and triple check that you have included all the appropriate pages and appendices, and use a cover memo to distinguish this version from prior versions, as well as to focus on the areas for special attention.

Q. Do you know when the summer session starts?

I do not love this question. Nor do I love its cousins referencing fall, winter session or spring. If you can find the information on the university website, please don't ask your committee member. I had to look it up the same way this student could have.

Questions before the Proposal

Q. My Lit Review has quite a bit of secondary sources. Can I leave them in and add information from the primary sources they refer to or should I get rid of the secondary sources all together and only use the primary?

Great question! So, the bigger question is, how did we get to this place? What I saw in this question is that the student in question has grown. Initially, he/she didn't know that there was an expectation to use primary, peer-reviewed sources for their review of the literature. While that makes a part of my heart sad, I can get over it, because he/she now knows what to do, and where these sources are found.

If the primary source was what the secondary source used to make the point, and the secondary source does not offer anything substantively new, then the primary source alone is sufficient. The student could leave the secondary source in, but it will look like he/she is padding the references list, so it is best to remove it. If the secondary source adds something substantive, then it is deserving of a citation and ought to remain.

Q. What are your thoughts on [the comment made by a committee member to strike a section]? Should I remove it or leave it?

This appears similar to the earlier question where one person liked a section and the other didn't, leaving the student confused. This question is from a tired student who is essentially asking me to tell him/her what to do. My advice:

set it all aside for a couple of days, then reread it with fresh eyes.

If it was a situation where the student was confused rather than tired I would offer a different answer, actually two, depending on the student's learning style preference. If the student is a more linear thinker, I would suggest backwards outlining that chapter to see how everything fits together. If that section was a digression, hopefully the student will see that in the backwards outline. If the student is a less linear thinker, I would suggest revisiting the concept map to see how integral the section is. Basically, I will refuse to make the decision, but instead, coach the student so that he/she can decide.

Q. What happens if I don't hear from the people who wrote the survey I want to use? Neither one is at the institutions they were at in 2006 when the article came out. I've tracked them each to different jobs and emailed to those places—one came back as not in the directory for that place—the other hasn't bounced back but hasn't been answered either....AACCKKK!! What should I do?

Take a deep breath. This student did not take a deep breath, he/she researched and found the authors' home phone numbers. While realizing that this was borderline stalking (also a funny email), the student did not call the authors at home. He/she did eventually get a reply from one of them at a business email.

If you find that the authors of the instrument you want to use are unavailable (after all, people don't live forever) see if it has been published by a publisher. While it may cost you money to use the instrument, you will be able to get the letter you need to include in your appendices this way. If the author of the instrument is deceased and no publisher is involved, and you *really* want to use that instrument, reach out to the institution where the author worked and see if the institution has a policy for dealing with these requests and who, if anyone, can authorize your use of the instrument in question. While this is going on, do start developing a plan B.

Q. Do I need to put my IRB approval letters in the Appendices?

Yes.

Questions about Data and Data Analysis

Q. I was thinking about what happens if I don't have enough volunteers for interviews. What do you think about submitting the questions in open-ended online survey format?

If you modify the data collection plan, then you will have to seek an IRB modification. Also, it is important to consider that an interview and a survey are not the same. Even if the survey questions are identical to the interview questions, the methods are not the same and will, therefore, have to analyzed differently. That is not a bad thing, but it is something to consider.

Q. How do I eliminate a portion of the sample from the testing?

First, why? If you have included the individuals in your sample, then why are you seeking to remove them? If you find that there is another characteristic muddying your data, then add the appropriate delimitation in chapters one and rationale in chapter three, but remember you will need to discuss the impact of this delimitation and any others in chapter five.

Q. Total N=1198, 25 responses. 2%, should I send out a reminder? (The survey launched Thursday, 2-13, and the email arrived Friday, 2-14.)

No! The bold is not a typo. I think the student's eagerness is awesome, but under no circumstances should you rend a reminder after one day. If you have so much energy that you need to do something, change the tense in chapter three to the past tense, that ought to hold you for a while. Finished with that and you still have to wait for more data? Ok, update your references, something was probably published in the month since you last revised it. If those suggestions sound snarky, it is because they are! Research can not be rushed.

So, the larger question remains: how frequently can you send a reminder and not be a pest? Whether you need to send a reminder at all may be a function of the length of your survey, the perceived value of the survey, the number of other surveys requested, when you sent it (Is it a busy time of year?), whether there is an incentive to complete the survey, and how likable you are in the invitation to participate. Maybe one reminder after ten days or two weeks, but take care not to send it to the people who participated.

I believe the person in question sent multiple reminders to the point where a couple of people took the time to call the IRB office. At that point the data collection was done, but (at least for me) the lesson was learned. I need to explicitly discuss with students conducting research that you should never abuse email addresses by sending multiple reminders.

Q. How the heck do I analyze this?

Heh. Um. Yeah. This email was sent to me by a student. My inside voice had a whole lot of answers, but my outside voice suggested that the student follow the data analysis plan laid out in chapter three.

Q. I do own an SPSS license and would be interested in running the appropriate test. Which one would you recommend?

Not the same student, but I did give a very similar answer. Before any student begins to collect data, he/she proposes a detailed data analysis plan that a committee approves in a very formal way. I am not sure what happens, but I suspect data analysis plans are written as an exercise without considering whether the student is comfortable carrying out the plan he/she described.

I guess this is as good a place as any to remind you that the committee trusts you are going to collect data according to the data-gathering plan you have described in chapter three and analyze those data according to the data analysis plan that you proposed.

Q. I want to triangulate data, I've read NUMEROUS article supporting it for validity and reliability…but is there a way you ACTUALLY PHYSICALLY TRIANGULATE the data? DO you correlate it? Create a linear relationship? Compare? I am missing something here and I don't see how triangulation is done and presented!

Everyone talks a good game around triangulation, but this student's question is a reminder that if faculty assume students know something going in, misconceptions can flourish. I am confident that this very capable student did well in his/her qualitative research course, but I am just as sure that knowing triangulation is important was stressed over actually triangulating data. Let me be specific, there is no physical triangulation.

Triangulation refers to using multiple (at least three: *tri*) forms and sources of data to address the same topic. In this way you can confirm or refute that each source of data is consistent with the others. If your data are in agreement, then you can draw conclusions based on the triangulated data. If your data are inconsistent, then you will need to seek more sources of data to answer your research question(s). Additionally, you will then explore what factors caused the data that you thought would be similar to be different.

Q. Doing another careful reread this morning of chapters 4 and 5 to remind myself of all the little things. I realized that I did not consistently offer an effect size. Am I right in saying that every time there is a "significant difference" in the results, I should cite an effect size also?

Yes.

144

Questions about Writing Results, Discussion, and Conclusion

Q. A quick question about tense (which has been my weakness is writing as far back as I can remember). Now, at this point, the methodology should be past tense, right? The whole thing should be past tense except the discussion? And the discussion will move between past and present depending on what I am referencing, right?

For the most part, this person is exactly right. In general, the dissertation reports on research that has been completed. Even chapter two reports on research that has been completed. In chapter five there will be a mix of past tense for what you found, possible present tense, or past tense for what it means depending on what you are discussing, and future tense for any recommendations regarding future research.

Q. The research question has a second level heading, then the question. Should I write "Findings" and then give the direct finding? Or just put it under the question without its own heading?

You do not need to include a findings subhead directly under the question you are answering. The findings chapter is organized by research question(s) and further by the other organizational structures which you have imposed on your dissertation in the writing of the earlier chapters. There is a more detailed description of how you can organize this section in chapter eight of this text.

Q. If I want to talk about something numerically in chapter 5, I must present it in chapter 4, right? So if I want to mention that the withdraw rate is alarming, I can not present the data for the first time in chapter 5.

True. This student is absolutely correct. No new data are presented in chapter 5, everything has to be mentioned in chapter 4 if you want to discuss it in chapter 5.

Q. If I talk about the data in Chapter 5, should I always just refer to Chapter 4? Or should I follow some of my points in Chapter 5 with numerical data. As in mean scores or t values.

If they have been presented in chapter 4 you are covered and can merely refer back to chapter 4, but since your goal is readability, if it will help the reader to have you include a number parenthetically here or there, do include it. If you want to refer to table 12 where all the data that you are using can be found, but table 12 is in chapter 4, then you will just include the table reference, not a copy of the table (Table 12) or (see Table 12).

Q. If I mention something in chapter 5, does it have to also be in chapter 2? Can I introduce anything – concept wise- for the first time in chapter 5?

The way this question is worded, no. If there are references that support the concept that you are thinking of introducing, and something was raised by your findings, then you go back into chapter 2 and find a way to weave the new concept in. If, on the other hand, the finding is anomalous, and there really is not literature base, then you can raise it as an area for future research. There is a bit more on this in chapter 9 of this document.

Q. I am a bit confused about delimitation/limitations. As of now, I have those in Chapters 1,3 and now 5. Is that correct? And I assume they all vary slightly?

They all vary quite a bit in how they are presented, but each limitation and delimitation does need to show up in all three of the chapters mentioned. In chapter one, you introduce the limitations and delimitations. Basically, you briefly call them out. In chapter three, you provide the rationale for each delimitation and the reason for each limitation. Wherever possible, you cite references to support your claims. Then, in chapter five, you discuss the possible implications of each of your limitations and delimitations. Here, too, you want to be

146

grounded in empirical research as much as possible. Thus, they are in all three chapters, but in different ways.

Questions about All the Other Stuff

Q. How can I get the page numbers right? There is no easy way to get them to be included WITHIN the margins that I can find, so I increase the footer to exist at 1.25in rather than .5in. I don't think it really shifted my pages…so I am not sure if its right!

Microsoft Word is mean. Not really, but that is the first answer I give to any page number or table format question I get. This student has described a work-around for the problem that does appear to work. The graduate school expectation for this student was that the 1" bottom margin was clean, no page number. The solution of setting the margin to 1.25" created a 1" clean margin, so it worked out perfectly!

Q. For the defense, I was going to pick up a Box of Joe and donuts and bagels, is that ok? Or should I do juice and fruit and veggie platters?

The defense is not about food. Yes, the student does usually bring something, but it doesn't matter what. Passing will not be dependent on whether it was bagels or fruit. Do avoid allergens. It would be unfortunate to inadvertently kill one of your committee members at the defense because they were allergic to nuts and you served a nut laden snack. I don't see how you could get them to sign off on your work if they were dead.

Q. I know you and I have briefly discussed this, but can you let me know how to go about ordering a cap and gown to buy?

Great question, because it means that the student has not only completed his or her work, but is celebrating the achievement by attending graduation. There are lots of places online to purchase your regalia, and on my campus you can actually purchase it at the bookstore too! So after a quick Google search, I see oakhalli.com, gradshop.com, graduationmall.com, and others. Note that there is a color difference for EdD and PhD degrees.

Q. If I present only, can the data then be used for a later publication submission?

Yes, it would only be double-dipping if there was a conference proceeding associated with the presentation.

Q. Now that my proposal was accepted for a roundtable, what do I do?

Celebrate! Congratulations. You don't have to do more than register for the conference and attend. It is a good idea to figure out how you want to describe your project and if you have any questions; you may want to type those up so you have them ready. The roundtable is a relatively informal way to present.

If you want, and this is truly optional, you can have a handout. This might give the other people at the roundtable greater ease in engaging with your ideas and might generate more discussion for you. If you do decide to make a handout, there are rarely more than 12 people at a table, so bringing 20 copies to the conference is more than enough.Make sure your contact information is on the handout in case someone has a thought or idea they can share with you later.

Chapter 12: Advice from Those Who Have Finished!

Following is a collections of letters to you, the doctoral student, as you work towards completing your degree. Each of these letters was solicited because the individual writer has a perspective that may be of use to you. Some are anonymous, others signed, but all were written by people who have finished the degree and lived to tell the tale. These individuals are caring practitioners who were willing to share a bit of their experience and some advice.

Capitalizing on Multiple Perspectives

Dear Doctoral Student,

Congratulations on your decision to further your education and obtain your doctoral degree. The path ahead of you may feel daunting or overwhelming at this moment, but with determination and support this can be such a rewarding journey. I know, because I walked this path also.

I began working on my doctorate in Educational Leadership in 2012. I actually had applied two years earlier, but with two young children at home and a full time job as a Senior Lecturer in Chemistry, I delayed my start date. I was unsure that I was doing the right thing for my career and family, so I turned down the acceptance. Two years later I had no doubt that I chosen the right path for my future and the faculty within the program were there to support me and help me get started. I chose my program because it offered the flexibility I needed while allowing me to tailor the degree to fit my interests. I was inspired by the coursework ahead and determined to pursue my degree with fervor, but there are some things I wish I had known when I started. That is what I would like to share with you.

First, the coursework; it is difficult to imagine choosing a dissertation topic so early into your educational process but stay focused on your interests. Use these interests and weave them throughout your coursework so that when you arrive at your dissertation, you have investigated it from many different facets along the way; through an organizational leadership perspective, through a policy perspective and a research perspective. If you feel passionate about a topic and have examined it critically, your dissertation work will be that much more comprehensive down the road. This multi-perspective approach in my own work resulted in three different publications in scholarly peer-review journals and a presentation at a regional conference, all different themes extracted from my final dissertation work.

Also, approach your coursework in an organized fashion, almost as if you are collecting data! Many of the ideas will weave together and overlap from course to course. Consider how you want to collect all the information, concepts and the readings. For me, that was in the form of a large electronic table that allowed me to track main ideas, quotes, authors and know where I had filed electronic copies within my database. When it came time to take my Comprehensive Exam and write my dissertation, this made retrieving all the information much easier.

Second, create a support network within your cohort. Make friends, get phone numbers and break bread together. These are the people who will understand your struggles ahead and will help pick you up and encourage you along the way when you feel too overwhelmed to keep going. They will be your lifeline and become your life long friends because of this journey.

Finally, enjoy the process. Take it all in. Smile at the fact that you are pursuing the highest level of education and working to become an expert in your field. Know that you have an incredible challenge ahead, but also know that you will never have the support and guidance that you do when you are submersed in this program. Use the expertise of your professors to make yourself a better educator, researcher or leader, because the rewards of this journey are sweet.

Wishing you strength and perseverance,

Tiffany L. Hesser, Ed.D. Educational Leadership

Facing Challenges

Dear Doctoral Student,

As you are well aware, the doctorate program is challenging. After all, you are getting two fancy letters to forever replace the honorifics that precede your name. I embraced the rigorous challenge of coursework, comprehensive exams and an eventual dissertation when I entered the doctoral program, unaware of the true challenges that were ahead of me.

It was quite the task to complete all the required competencies and coursework to be granted the seal of approval to begin writing my dissertation while keeping my head above water at work. I was the head of a large program for minority students in a large urban district. I had 25 bosses; I had my direct report to answer to, and then on top of that the principals of each and every building in the district, not to mention board members, community groups, parents and teachers who needed my support and assistance. Days were always super challenging, and I always felt like crisis occurred while I was in class focusing on my personal pursuits. I was supposed to have my phone off and be in tune with the content

151

of instruction provided by instructors who were trying to help me gain the golden ring to be able to begin the dissertation process. Classes were after work hours, but somehow work never had a closing bell. I felt like Gumby, I was pulled in several directions at one time, and wondered when I would be stretched so thin I would snap. There were signs of this all around. My house was a mess, my dog was terribly misbehaving from lack of attention, and my friendships suffered. Then, a shock came to the program I was attending as the inspirational leader of my doctoral program fell ill and after a short period passed away. Programs move on, as they do, and he was replaced by someone who did not share his philosophy. Much of the work I had done up to this point had to be redone- and the new leader of the program was very clear on the fact that I would not receive the magic ticket of graduating unless I followed his new direction. This is not to say that the new direction was wrong- it was just different and another step to add which made the ladder to program completion even more difficult to climb. I accepted the changes and plugged on.

Then, the unthinkable happened. My job was cut. I now had a new set of worries, a new set of stressors, and a new distraction to my work. Depression ensued. I felt a lack of self-worth, and the challenge of getting out of bed, never mind completing a dissertation.

I questioned myself. I questioned my motivations. Losing my job made me question what I knew and why I was in a doctoral program to begin with.

I was lost, and had to find myself.

I accepted a position several levels below the one I once had. I was supervised by those who I once supervised. I once sat at the head of the table at and now I was barely invited to innovative committees in my field of work.

I had to figure out my way and was terribly shamed by the experience.

It was now common for me to sleep in on the weekends as losing my position meant that I had to take on various extra jobs just to break even. I can still remember the day that I woke up and all of a sudden an elephant was not stepping on my chest. It was a typical weekend day- only, something was different about the day. I had done so much- I had come so far. I had invested several years in to a program that I was going to be indebted to pay back student loans on for the next 25 years, whether I completed it or not. I couldn't fail at this- I had to complete what I had started. I stopped fighting with myself, and started working with myself. This meant listening to me. Novel concept, right? My only weekend plan was me. I slept when I wanted to, I gave myself dog walking breaks- and I found a clarity that I had been lacking.

I had forgotten a lot of the work I had done; authors were mushed together in my mind, and while I knew the popular theories, I couldn't remember what theory came from where. My experience started with me getting back to where I was. I reread several articles, and as I did so, new articles appeared. I then opened the new articles, and built upon my understanding. Connections that were once at best fuzzy became in focus. However, there was something very different about this time as I did the reading on my own terms. I read when I wanted to, took breaks when I needed to, and gave myself personal deadlines versus the ones that had been previously set by my program. The physical space I used was even different, as before I used to work in my office- and since I no longer had my old job I got out of working on my dissertation by using the excuse that I had no location to get the work done. To put this excuse to bed, I knocked out a closet door (which now I complain about losing the storage space), and made myself a nook where there were no surrounding distractions. This nook was like the casino philosophy where I wasn't able to determine the time of day and therefore did not stop working when I was on a roll simply because it was dinner or bed time. I basically learned to listen to myself. When I got to a place in my work where I felt I was going in circles, I literally walked away, and then came back hours or even days later. I printed up one of those big calendars that typically fill a desk. On the calendar, I made small goals. I wrote when certain chapters would be complete or dreaded formatting. I then held myself accountable by emailing my chair and told her that the work would be there on the dates I set. In between, I allowed myself to have breaks such as days with a friend or hikes with my dog. However, I called those due dates "done dates" as I could take as many breaks as I wanted as long as work was done by the date I set.

Through re-focusing on my dissertation I gained confidence that I had lost. I once again felt like an expert in my field and this gave me the energy to continue.

There wasn't any specific article I read. There wasn't any specific training I went to. I wish it was as easy as telling you to watch an inspirational movie or go to some conference. It is more about a personal journey. Listen to yourself. Give yourself what you need. Look at what you have accomplished from the start of your program to where you are right now instead of feeling lost in what is left to be completed. And remember, once you complete your program, no one can ever take your golden ticket away. You will be reminded of what you accomplished every time you hear someone address you by your well- earned title of "Doctor".

Sincerely,

Dr. Survivor

New Job and New Family

Dear Doctoral Student,

I writing to you to let you know that you have embarked on the most rewarding journey of your educational career. The process is not easy and your professional and personal life do not stop. There are plenty reasons to explain why only 1.68% of Americans have doctoral degrees; the process is a true test to see if you have a desire, persistence, and perseverance. The road is filled with twists and turns, I can tell you it is an unbelievable feeling of accomplishment to get called back in after your dissertation defense and your advisor says, "Dr....can you come back into the room?"

I signed up with the third doctoral cohort with 24 other students. We all started the journey together and provided support, laughter, and friends to commiserate with. This is not a process for the faint of heart, this road has many unexpected detours. I hit many bumps in the road during my studies and I will detail only a few. I felt like I was really moving along in my study of school discipline, I had secured a school district that allowed me access to their student discipline data and as I progressed with my action research; it revealed that this district was not reporting their discipline data properly and the state came in to provide oversight and restructure their administration. This was extremely disheartening and was a major setback. Shortly after this setback, I took on an administrative job at one of the largest high schools in Connecticut – and I would not let anything prevent me from finishing but I needed to regroup and reassess my situation. If things couldn't get complicated enough, I got engaged to a foreign national (immigration nightmare) and was married a year later. I know what you are thinking, this guy is crazy and what is he trying to do? As I said this process makes you dig deep into yourself and determine is this something you really want to do. When I found out that my wife was pregnant with a baby girl; that sent me into serious focus mode and I really

155

buckled down and made the decision to get this completed because Daddy needs to finish what he started. I even remember sending my final edits to my dissertation advisor from the hospital nursery – after the birth of my daughter. What I really want you to understand is that things happen along the way, life happens and no one expects you to put your life on hold but they will be there to help you manage and get through the process. I received lots of "tough love" from all of the readers on my dissertation and they wanted to cut me loose if I wasn't serious. I know that sounds rough but it was what I needed to get myself motivated and moving in the right direction.

I would happily tell you my tale and share more stories about the doctoral program, the doctoral comp exam, the dissertation writing process, and dissertation defense. I would ask you to clear your calendar for a couple of hours and I hope the diner offers a bottomless cup of coffee. I want to let you know that you are not alone in this endeavor and you are able to reach out to staff and students to lift you up when you fall or feel like you can't continue. It isn't easy BUT it is rewarding beyond measure. My hope for you is that you are able to enjoy the pleasure of holding the highest degree attainable in your given field. I wish you all the best, continued success and I hope you complete the race (no one cares what place you come in – as long as you finish the race).

Your sympathetic friend,

Joseph DiBacco, Ed.D.

P.S.

Here is something that I found helpful:

Believe it or not using Google Scholar was very helpful; I used it to see how many times and author was referenced or how many times a research article was linked to another resource...this really helped me dig deeper and determine seminal pieces of research...it also helped me see the authors that kept reappearing…I knew I needed to read their research…I hope that helps…please reach out if needed!!

A Transformative Journey

Dear Doctoral Student,

Confucius once said *"Jump….and the net will appear!"*. If you are a doctoral student deeply immersed in your work, carefully consider this: The process of pursuing – and ultimately completing – a doctoral dissertation is a complex and transformative one. Successfully navigating a doctorate requires a special kind of resilience, courage, and unrelenting drive that borders on believing in things not yet visible or fully realized – hence, a call to believe in a net that has yet to materialize. To that end, I would like to take a few moments to offer some advice on how you might deal with the emotional aspects of finishing your dissertation.

My own journey as a doctoral student began nearly 3 decades ago, but I recall the experience vividly, with all its ups and downs. In my current role as a professor in an educational leadership doctoral program, I work with doctoral candidates in various stages of their course and dissertation work. Additionally, for the past 3 years, I have been conducting research on the post-dissertation phase for Ed.D. students, where the transition from student to doctoral graduate presents myriad rewards, joys, angst, and challenges. The juxtaposition of my personal experiences as a doctoral student, my professional capacity as a teacher and advisor to current doctoral students, and my role as a researcher regarding the Ed.D. doctoral experience positions me to speak to you specifically regarding the unique emotional journey you may be experiencing now.

Earning your doctorate is unlike almost any other educational journey you have or will undertake. Your initial expectations and assumptions may drastically change by the time you complete this degree. If there is one thing I can tell you with certainty, it is this: Whoever you were when you started your doctoral program, you will not resemble that person by the time you finish your program. The transformation process is profound, deeply felt, and disruptive; you think you are just entering yet another degree program and you approach the work with ambition and determination. What happens to you while you are pursuing your goals is a shift in your identity, your confidence, your professional orientation, your ability to frame a problem and your ability to articulate its context, as well as the shifts in your personal relationships and your connection to your personal responsibilities. There is a sense of accomplishment balanced by a strange sense of loss; there is a sense of shifting priorities balanced by a need for a connection with others just like yourself. You may feel that your ability to complete the work seems elusive some days ... while on other days, you are filled with a sense of clarity and focus. While all of this sounds wonderful, the effects on you and on those around you are more complicated. As one of my study participants noted, "you are simply NOT the same person when you're done!", and the emotional baggage that comes with this knowledge is sometimes difficult to manage. If you feel increasingly challenged about your work-life balance, your time management abilities, your increasing interest in research studies and your decreasing interest in things you used to love .... you are not alone!

But here is the good news about all this transformation, much of which has happened or is happening to you when you weren't looking.... there is a happy ending! While the transformation is not without some angst, the growth process always stretches us and I promise that the effort is worth the turbulence. There are numerous ways you can manage this transformative journey and often they are very personal, but I would like to offer a few basic activities to stay sane and positive:

158

- **Don't be afraid to ask**...for help, advice, direction, resources, technical assistance! The educational doctorate is a doctorate of collaboration and community – your advisor(s), faculty, librarians, technicians, and fellow students are as much a part of your work as you are of theirs. Do not suffer in silence and isolation – reach out!

- **Stay connected** to your fellow students on a regular basis, as they best understand what you are experiencing; venting and sharing are important ways to de-stress and identify new approaches to your work.

- Do not view discouragement or anxiety about your work negatively, but rather see these feelings as part of the **growth process** – you cannot grow and evolve if you do not stumble. Many participants in my study expressed that the times when they felt the greatest discouragement about their work were the times when they had a significant breakthrough in writing, research, or analysis.

- **Be patient** with family, friends, and co-workers who may not understand what your program is really like for you; for many of them, this is just another degree program, just one homework assignment, just one more paper. While you may not be able to explain exactly what you are doing, you need their love and compassion, their support and their understanding. Offer them your patience in return. You cannot do this alone!

- **Take time** each week for yourself, to reflect, read, think about something other than the doctorate; a little distance from the Ed.D. will actually help you be more productive and focused. Many of my participants found that keeping a journal was therapeutic and helpful in debriefing some difficult periods in their processes.

- To that point, **physical activity and exercise** are essential to your mental acuity and energy, and the release of stress and anxiety will be more helpful than you can imagine.

A brisk walk around your block will benefit you more than a second bowl of ice cream!

In closing, please remember that you are part of a very special group of people who are pursuing a terminal degree. Managing your emotional challenges during this process are a means to a very significant end – earning a doctorate and an opportunity to give back to the world around you in positive and meaningful ways. To make the most of that opportunity, you need to emerge from this process as a strong, compelling, and wholly transformed individual.

All the best as you complete your program,

Felice D. Billups, Ed.D.

Been There, Done That!

Dear Doctoral Student,

I don't know you and you don't know me. Yet, we have a common thread that binds us: the pursuit of a doctoral degree. You may be content with the certainty that you were born to pursue and receive this degree. Or, you may be like me, driven to do this but uncertain that you will be smart enough, dedicated enough, talented enough, to realize this dream. You may be juggling a family and a career. You may be taking a sabbatical from your career for this. Or, you may be like me, setting out on this path with very few demands on your time. Regardless of our differences, we all have the same goal in mind.

If you don't have a topic in mind, begin thinking of one as soon as you receive that acceptance letter. If you have an idea of the general areas of your interest you can use it to focus the time, energy, and effort you put into your early papers so that your dissertation has a solid background or so that you have time to explore a vast body of research related to your area of interest. Don't wait until the end of your second year to begin thinking of a topic. By then, you will have missed

160

the opportunity to use two full years worth of papers as research time. It may not seem to be a huge deal right now but, later, you'll wish you had been more focused and strategic in your use of time.

The road to completing the doctoral degree is long. The road is windy and there are many, many pitfalls, twists, and turns. You may sit in your first semester's classes and feel as if you are not nearly as smart as everyone else and that, one day, everyone will realize it and laugh at you. You may fear that your professors will tear your writing to shreds. Don't worry, they will. But they won't do it in front of everyone and they won't do it to be mean. They'll do it because they care and because they want you to write effectively and concisely. If they don't do this, then you should push yourself to improve your writing. You need to be your biggest critic when it comes to your writing. If you aren't, then your dissertation will take forever and may very well turn out to be something that you are ashamed to have published. Don't be ashamed of your hard work; publish it so others can read it!

There may be emergencies and life events that arise during the course of your studies. I struggled with a mother who was 800 miles away and battling an extremely rare auto-immune disorder for which there was no treatment. In between working, coaching, and taking classes, I would book flights and leave my dog with a friend every Friday afternoon and return late Sunday night. Why? Because my mother was my biggest cheerleader, my biggest critic, and my rock. No matter how many times she and my father told me to stay home and focus on my studies, I boarded that plane every Friday for six months.

You'll feel as if you have no life, and you'll be absolutely correct. Your friends will be an afterthought. You'll spend your time focusing on the immense amount of reading and rather vague guidelines for papers and projects. If you're married, your spouse and family (if you have one) will have to adjust to a new reality for a few years because you won't be there as much and, even if you are there, you will be busy with study groups and schoolwork. You will need to learn to balance loving your family/spouse/significant other and loving yourself. You will need to set aside time for your studies, your research, your writing. Don't worry, you won't be shortchanging your children. Instead, you'll be setting an amazing example of discipline, structure, and lifelong learning. Speaking of study groups, form one in your first semester. Don't pick and choose, don't cherrypick. Make the study group open to everyone and then be certain to evenly distribute the work. Those who don't pull their own weight are no longer welcome. Does it seem a bit cutthroat? Maybe it is. But you need to remember that there is no reason to enable others to benefit from the hard work of others, at the same time, everyone who is wiling to do their share is welcome! Many hands make light work, and everyone can be successful if they do the work.

Somewhere down the line, you may realize that the dissertation topic you once thought was brilliant is no longer your passion. That's okay. You can refine it. But please don't veer completely away from it. If you do, all of your hard work and the plethora of papers you've already written on the topic will all be for naught and you'll have to start from nothing. Don't do that. Starting over can be the reason you have a harder time finishing. Don't be an ABD. Be an Ed.D. or a Ph.D.!

When it comes time to consider your committee, choose wisely! You need to choose a sponsor and committee members who will not only be your critics but also your colleagues. Your sponsor needs to be your biggest critic but also your friend. Don't choose someone with whom you are not completely comfortable. Choose someone whose background and interests are somewhat similar to yours, but not too similar. If you choose a committee member whose research interests are exactly the same as yours, you'll run the risk of being pressured to replicate his/her research. Then, you'll have to have that really awkward conversation with the department chair about replacing that committee member with someone else. Try not to pick the same sponsor as many other people because that sponsor likely won't have the time to dedicate to your research. And that's not okay. You and your research deserve (and need) someone who is willing to put in a significant amount of time and work into making your research a quality item, regardless of physical location of the sponsor.

Don't hoard your research. Share it with your peers. Share it with your colleagues. Remember that study group from the first semester? It may be down to only a few members by now but stay in touch with them. You should all be supporting each other and sharing any and all research that can help you. These people are your tribe, your support system. You may be lucky enough to find one particular person in that initial study group who ends up being your buddy. If you do, plan your program and courses together. Try to go through as much of the coursework as you can together. There's nothing like starting and graduating with someone.

Somewhere in the craziness, I meet someone and start dating. In under one year, as I was writing my dissertation, I got engaged, took a new job, built a new house, started a new job, planned a wedding, got married, and then got pregnant. When life gets that crazy, you just need to keep going. You need to set aside time to write. It may not be easy to find large blocks of time and that's fine. Even if you can write an hour a day, three or four days a week, you'll be in great shape. The more you write, the sooner you can send things to your sponsor and the sooner everything will be revised and ready for the critical comments of your committee members. And they will have comments, which is wonderful because you will know that they not only read your research but also thought about it and cared enough about it (and you) to try to make it better.

Your sponsor may not understand the many things in your life. Or your sponsor may use them as a reason for you to slow down. Or your sponsor could be as amazing as mine: be completely understanding but still urging you on to finish and finish quickly. Getting pregnant with my first child lit a fire under me like nothing else ever could. When it came to nailing down a defense date that worked for everyone, I was willing to push it back a month because I was still going to be able to defend a day before my due date. My sponsor put her foot down and found a way for me to defend towards the end of the semester. And good thing she did because my daughter was born a week early. My first congratulatory phone call came from my buddy from my doctoral program. She had defended her dissertation that morning. We began together and we finished together!

Been there, done that, earned the degree,

Niralee Patel-Lye

Being a A New ABD Hire at a University

Dear Rising Colleague,

Congratulations on this important step of your career! If you are considering taking a full time job in academia, you will have an exciting new platform for sharing your knowledge and expertise with others. While it is helpful that the responsibilities of your new job are similar to those of finishing your dissertation, remember that *many additional* tasks will be asked of your time. You will have to dedicate yourself to meeting the expectations of two different jobs.

Before offering recommendations on balancing the responsibilities of completing a dissertation and full-time employment in academia, let me share a bit about myself. I am an Assistant Professor in Communication Disorders and am fortunate to teach our undergraduate and graduate students. I also supervise graduate students in our clinic. I was offered this

164

tenure track position shortly after finishing data collection for my dissertation. While my dean and chair provided release time to support continued work on my dissertation, much of my first year was spent preparing materials for the new (to me) courses I covered. With minimal teaching experience, I underestimated the time needed to prepare for and deliver material. I also had a limited understanding of the additional responsibilities related to committee work, grant writing, and other documentation associated with the position.

Now beyond my year as a new ABD hire, here are a few tips that I hope will support you as you consider taking a new position. Overall, in managing your responsibilities, be *truthful* and *realistic*! While you will certainly give all you can to your new position and inwardly want to believe you can do it all (and excellently at that), do not assume you will get it all done. Do not assume that unscheduled periods of time will be naturally devoted to finishing your dissertation. Rather, schedule and protect regular blocks of time for your dissertation. If possible, schedule blocks that are three or more hours, as you will find it often takes time to mentally put aside the responsibilities and commitments of your other job and re-enter the writing process. Also consider advertising to your colleagues the periods of time that you are working on your dissertation and any personal/university-level deadlines in place for writing. In agreeing to hire you ABD, your colleagues and department are committed to you successfully completing your dissertation. While they would certainly appreciate your more immediate availability, knowing that you will continue to serve your university in upcoming years is a much greater payoff for their investment.

Finally, remember that you are your greatest advocate. While there are performance expectations for new hires, you know your strengths and areas for growth. You understand the levels of stress under which you can be academically productive and the environments that best foster your development. Strive to create a schedule that promotes *your* success while incorporating the responsibilities of a doctoral candidate and full-time professor.

Wishing you all the best and a successful future,

Hillary V. Harper, Ph.D., CCC-SLP

Prioritize Daily

Dear Doctoral Student,

The process of writing your dissertation can seem daunting and challenging, but imagine you are knee deep in data analysis when...things outside of your control change. For me, the common challenges of procrastination, isolationism, and perfectionism were not the ones that affected me most as I completed my dissertation. Big changes in my career and professional life could have very easily taken me way off course as I worked to complete dissertation.

My name is Jessica Pawlik-York and I enjoyed the process of completing my dissertation, but it was not without some obstacles, stress, and decision-making. I am person who truly believes that the only constant in life is change. The stress of changes going on around you can greatly influence your ability to sit down and grind out sentences, paragraphs, and data analysis. What I could have never planned for were the unexpected changes that would unfold in my professional life as I moved though the process of completing my dissertation.

I never intended to apply for jobs while completing my dissertation, but I began to get curious about what was out there in my field. Rather quickly, I had applied for a dream job and was offered the position. My entire life changed. I worked much longer hours, juggled times my young children, and had to somehow find time to complete my dissertation. There were many nights where I swear I actually heard my pillow calling out my name, but I was probably hearing things from being overtired.

Before I could understand how much changing my job would affect my ability to complete my dissertation, nearly a month had gone by. I was so excited and wrapped up in my new job that I almost lost sight of the finish line. My supervisor invited me into her office and asked me one simple question, "how do you plan and prioritize what you need to do on a daily basis?" The truth is that I could not answer that question. I thought long and hard about this question over many days and was struck by three important realizations that would drive me to complete my dissertation: commitment, do what you say you will do, and never leave something for tomorrow that you can do today.

Personal drive and commitment drove me to work on completing my dissertation. I set a realistic goal date of when I wanted to complete certain tasks and held myself accountable. This allowed me to have a number of smaller goals as I completed my dissertation. I was able to keep my work and family obligations, while feeling rewards for completing tasks. Committing to doing what you say you will do is challenging. While its not a guarantee, really living this way will cause you think much more purposefully about things in life. When I say I will do something, I do it. No if, ands, or buts. If something can be done today, do it. Leaving something until tomorrow increases the likelihood of it not being done. For me this is especially true. I know that if I delay something that should be done today, tomorrow is not a guarantee.

The key to my advice is not to follow the steps that got me through my dissertation amidst some serious changes in my professional life, but rather that you take the time to figure out what is that will drive you to be successful in completing your work. Be realistic. Set goals. Keep moving forward.

Respectfully,

Jessica Pawlik-York, Ed.D.

Director of Education Programs, Post University

Chapter 13: Concluding Words

In pulling together a document like this I was struck by how much advice and just how many resources are available to a person writing his or her dissertation. It seems that a lot of it is "good advice that you just didn't take" (Morissette, 1996). In fact, reading everything that has been written about how to best complete a dissertation could derail you from actually completing your dissertation. No matter how good a strategy looks on paper, if it doesn't work for you, it isn't worthy of further consideration.

At the beginning of this text, I suggested that you would benefit from reflecting some and getting to know yourself. I don't take that back, I want to emphasize it. Play to your strengths. If you are a social person, find ways to be around people while you are working. Perhaps you benefit from friendly competition? Well then, ignore advice that suggests that you don't compare yourself to your colleagues, because for you that might work as a motivator.[26] I prefer to compete against myself, so the tracking features in any project management tool are helpful.

If you don't benefit from competition, but rather value a sense of community without comparisons, you may want to

---

[26] If you are using the KanbanFlow app, then you can compete based on your productivity with "friends". In your personal settings, you can enable the game feature and then it will rank you based on how much work you do. https://kanbanflow.com/settings/game

find a writing group where people are working on different types of writing projects. Sure, you are working on your dissertation, but someone else may be writing a novel and another person a children's book, and each of you will have common interests minus the comparable products. There are a lot of online writers groups, but you may even find one that meets in your area monthly or weekly. I know most of the towns in this area have groups such as these through their respective fine arts organizations.

What if your favorite company is a cup of tea or coffee while you are working? Then, don't try to change that, and don't join a writing group! If you need a little bit of extra structure consider a tool that helps you carve you time for your writing (there are many, including https://pacemaker.press/ and http://writetrack.davidsgale.com/ are just two). These tools encourage you to set goals and then help structure your writing time based on your past writing pace to meet your goal. Another neat tool (one of my friends from college used this to write his first novel) is National Novel Writing Month. During the month of November, http://nanowrimo.org/ offers support for your work, and the organizers have even added Camp Nanowrimo for months other than November. If you need a push, but don't want to fully interact with a writing group, consider this type of on-line support.

Tips for Anyone

There are some strategies that help nearly every writer, regardless of how you choose to work. These include chunking your task, celebrating successes, and finding your balance. Each of these will help you be successful, but you will still need to tailor it to your individual needs to get a perfect fit. Take what appears helpful and make it your own.

Chunking your task, at a minimum, involves considering each chapter as a separate entity. A chapter might be twenty pages or so; a much more manageable undertaking than the whole dissertation. For me, chunking is more extreme.

170

I look at each element of a dissertation as its own enterprise. This is particularly useful for chapter two. Using my concept map to create an outline, then each subhead of the outline becomes a brief paper that I approach. As an anxious writer, the though of pulling together a whole chapter was more than I could tolerate, and the stress this prospect caused me had me paralyzed.

It turns out that I can write a short research paper on a narrow topic without that paralytic anxiety. As I wrote the small research papers, I stayed focused and was able to ensure that I had a complete beginning, middle and end to the section, mainly because I considered it a paper which had to stand on its own. When I had a collection of these little papers, I arranged them in the order of my outline and added appropriate transitions between them. I found it easy to write a transition paragraph connecting the ideas from two already-completed sections. This was much easier than attempting to figure out how the ideas connected before I had written the mini-papers.

What the chunking did for me was allow me the space to dig deeply into each idea and fully consider it without having to take into account the larger picture. Only after I developed the smaller idea did I spend time reflecting on how it connected. This worked for me because I am digression-prone. If I tried to keep the larger context in focus, I would have become distracted by all the intricacies of the connections.

I did have to go back and make all these connections, as they are an essential part of the review of literature, and reporting the content of the subhead is as well. By chunking the task, I created a structure for my writing that was required to ensure I had not only addressed the content of the subheading, but also included the appropriate levels of analysis and synthesis.

The chunking also provided me with plenty of interim goals that I could celebrate. Not everyone needs as much external reward or goal tracking as I do, but it is important to know your needs and work with them. A celebration can be treating yourself to something or even just checking off the task as done. I used to make lists just so I could cross items off. Now I use a program that allows me to tick a box when a small task is completed and drag it to a "done" column when the larger project is finished. This is my reward.

Depending on your personal needs, establish your reward in advance of starting to work. This way you don't inflate the reward as you work, or change the goal on yourself. Structure your reward system based on the relative importance and desirability of tasks so that a less appealing task comes with a greater reward. For example, I enjoyed writing up my results, so writing a section of chapter four had a very small reward (checking a box) whereas I HATED working on chapters one and two. These sections merited a short walk or a nice luxurious bath.

Beware of rewards that will make you less healthy or rewards that end up making you feel worse. If you struggle to manage your weight, please do not reward yourself with calorie-rich food. I have a food-reward story for you. For finishing writing chapter two I decided to take myself out for a lobster dinner. Awesome! Being from New England, I learned to crack a lobster almost before I learned to read. I got my lobster and started to dig in, but my lips started to swell and I experienced a difficult time breathing. Damn it! Somewhere along the line of graduate school, when I couldn't afford a lobster, I developed an allergy. Clearly, I didn't die, but I associate my dissertation with my new food allergy.

I am in no way suggesting that if you reward yourself with food there will be dire consequences, but when you are already sitting more than you would normally, it doesn't seem like a good plan to build in lots of extra food. Use your rewards to treat your brain and body especially well for all the hard work they have put in.

172

The final strategy that I feel is universal is finding or keeping a balance between your dissertation work and your life. Everyone will have his/her own balance point. Some people have few external demands on their time and can commit to working on their dissertation 2-3 hours a day after work and 5-6 hours each weekend day. Some individuals will find that they can only work for an hour in the morning before their family wakes up and an hour after everyone goes to bed. Still others can't make it happen during the week, but have the freedom to devote 12+ hours each weekend day. Find your strategy and be consistent.

Something that helps implement this strategy is actively protecting your time in your calendar. Write the writing time in your calendar in ink, or schedule it digitally and don't move it for anything. The laundry will be there after you have done some writing. The time you designate for working on your dissertation is crucial to getting your work done. Don't schedule more time for this than you can reasonably spend, as this will force you to either become unbalanced in your dissertation/life equilibrium or complete other tasks during the time you dedicated to working on your dissertation. Once you start interrupting the time you scheduled for dissertation work, it becomes easier and easier to co-opt that time for other, more pressing, things.

Using some sort of project management system helps protect your time once you have set it up in your calendar. If all your tasks are laid out on a project board, then you can see what needs to get done and just jump in. You will not waste time figuring out what you need to do. A checklist is a low tech way to achieve the same goal. You can even use your outline as a checklist, crossing off items as they are addressed.

Finding your balance may require you to stop working even when it is going well. This can be very, very difficult. If you have a great flow going, stopping to eat or sleep can become a threat to your productivity. Nothing could be further from the truth! Without appropriate food and sleep your work will suffer, as will your health. If you get sick, your productivity will plummet, so do whatever you can to stay healthy, and that includes stopping to eat and going to bed at a reasonable hour.

Pulling It All Together

When you started reading this book I promised you that I would keep coming back to the analogy of building your research home. Your dissertation serves as your entrance into the academy, but also becomes a part of your identity. It is where you are "from". I hope when you choose your topic you considered the future you, the one who will have to answer "what was the topic of your dissertation?" over and over again. Unlike your hometown, or another descriptor of your early self, you have the power to select the starting point of your identity as an academic.

That is why surveying the landscape is so crucial to the early process of writing your dissertation. It would stink to build a beautiful house on a lot that is down-wind of a smelly manufacturing plant, or on a lot that frequently floods. Choosing the focus of your research defines your academic roots. An ill-considered topic or a hasty decision that you commit to too early can stifle your growth. If you think you have made a poor choice, take the time to look around for another plot of land before you continue building a research home in the wrong spot. Sure, it may slow you down a bit, but the time was not wasted if it brought you to the place you need to be.

Along each stage of building your research home you have not only the decisions of what to do, but also how well to do it. There are builder-grade materials, and then there are the materials that the builder would choose if he/she were building his or her own house. How long do you intend to be in academia? Do you need to or want to build a research home that will stand up to a storm of critique or withstand the

174

ravages of time? Then you will devote more time and energy creating a high-quality product. There are some that are not as invested in joining academia, but rather need the doctoral credential for career advancement in a related field. They need to build a mobile home dissertation. This creates some conflicts with the needs and desires of the student and the desires of the program to require work that meets a minimum standard. If you find yourself looking to build a mobile home, please make sure that the program you have chosen will permit that, or you may want to transfer as many credits as you can to a program that will.

I hope that at the end of your dissertation work, you have crafted a research home that represents you well, and that you have found your way to enjoy the process. You only get to earn your doctorate once, and so I beseech you to take every opportunity to engage fully with your content and the entire world that surrounds doctoral education. A rich community exists for those engaged in doctoral studies; enjoy your brief stay in that space while you build your research home!

References

Anseel, F., Lievens, F., & Levy, P. E. (2007). A self-motives perspective on feedback-seeking behavior: Linking organizational behavior and social psychology research. *International Journal of Management Reviews*, *9*(3), 211–236. http://doi.org/10.1111/j.1468-2370.2007.00210.x

Benner, T. (2014). Quiz: What Type of Writer Are You? (And How to Make It Work for Your Content). Retrieved from http://blog.influenceandco.com/quiz-what-type-of-writer-are-you-and-how-to-make-it-work-for-your-content

Billups, F. D. (2016). Jumping into the abyss: Life after the doctorate. In *Higher Education* (Vol. 22). Retrieved from http://scholarsarchive.jwu.edu/highered/22/?utm_source=schola rsarchive.jwu.edu%2Fhighered%2F22&utm_medium=PDF&ut m_campaign=PDFCoverPages

Cohen, J. (1992). A Power Primer. *Psychological Bulletin*, *112*(1), 155–159. http://doi.org/10.1037/0033-2909.112.1.155

Covey, S. R. (2004). *The 7 Habits of Highly Effective People. 7 Habits of Highly Effective People* (Vol. 1). New York: Free Press. http://doi.org/10.1108/00251749810245309

Creswell, J., & Clark, V. (2011). *Designing and conducting mixed-methods research. The Sage handbook of qualitative research.* Thousand Oaks, CA: Sage Publications.

Creswell, J. W. (1994). *Research design: Qualitative & quantitative approaches*. Thousand Oaks, CA: Sage Publications.

Creswell, J. W. (2014). *Research design: Qualitative, quantitative and mixed methods approaches*. Thousand Oaks, CA: Sage Publications.

Creswell, J. W., & Garrett, A. L. (2008). The "movement" of mixed methods research and the role of educators. *South African Journal of Education*, *28*, 321–333.

Creswell, J. W., & Miller, D. L. (2000). Determining validity in qualitative inquiry. *Theory into Practice*, *39*(3), 124–130.

Dweck, C. (2006). *Mindset: The new psychology of success*. New York: Ballantine Books.

Dweck, C., Chiu, C., & Hong, Y. (1995). Implicit theories and their role in judgments and reactions: A word from two perspectives. *Psychological Inquiry*. Retrieved from http://www.tandfonline.com/doi/abs/10.1207/s15327965pli0604_1

Fishbach, A., & Choi, J. (2012). When thinking about goals undermines goal pursuit. *Organizational Behavior and Human Decision Processes*, *118*(2), 99–107. http://doi.org/10.1016/j.obhdp.2012.02.003

Gregory, J. L. (2012). Concept mapping, finding your way. In B. P. Skott & M. Ward (Eds.), *Active Learning Exercises for Research Methods in Social Sciences*. Thousand Oaks, CA: Sage Publications.

Gregory, J. L. (2015). Can We Succeed if We Don't Speak the Same Language? by Jess Gregory. Retrieved August 11, 2016, from http://www.ajeforum.com/can-we-succeed-if-we-dont-speak-the-same-language-by-jess-gregory/

Grinyer, A. (2002). The anonymity of research participants: assumptions, ethics and practicalities. *Social Research Update*, (36). Retrieved from http://sru.soc.surrey.ac.uk/SRU36.html

Guba, E. G. (1990). *The paradigm dialog*. (E. G. Guba, Ed.). Newbury Park, CA: Sage.

Guba, E. G., & Lincoln, Y. S. (1994). Competing paradigms in qualitative research. In N. K. Denzin & Y. S. Lincoln (Eds.), *Handbook of qualitative research* (2nd ed., pp. 163–194). Thousand Oaks, CA: Sage Publications.

Hemingway, E., Seldes, G., Dreiser, T., Hughes, L., & Ficke, A. D. (1935, October). Monologue to the maestro: A high seas letter. *Esquire*. Retrieved from https://dianedrake.com/wp-content/uploads/2012/06/Hemingway-Monologue-to-the-Maestro1.pdf

Kolb, D. A. (1976). Management and the learning process. *California Management Review*, *18*(3), 21–31.

Lahman, M. K. E., Rodriguez, K. L., Moses, L., Griffin, K. M., Mendoza, B. M., & Yacoub, W. (2015). A Rose By Any Other Name Is Still a Rose? Problematizing Pseudonyms in Research. *Qualitative Inquiry*, *21*(5), 445–453. http://doi.org/10.1177/1077800415572391

Langer, E. (1997). *The power of mindful learning.* Retrieved from http://psycnet.apa.org/psycinfo/1997-97457-000

Langer, E. J., & Moldoveanu, M. (2000). The Construct of Mindfulness. *Journal of Social Issues, 56*(1), 1–9. http://doi.org/10.1111/0022-4537.00148

Laursen, L. (2008). No , You ' re Not an Impostor. *Science Careers, 15,* 8–10. Retrieved from http://www.impostorsyndrome.com/wp-content/uploads/2014/03/science02142008.pdf

Lederach, J. P. (2005). *The Moral Imagination.* New York: Oxford University Press. http://doi.org/10.1093/0195174542.001.0001

Lennon, J., & McCartney, P. (1967). All you need is love. In Beatles (Ed.), *Magical Mystery Tour.* London: Parlophone; Capitol Records.

Locke, L. F., Spirduso, W. W., & Silverman, S. J. (1987). *Proposals that work: A guide for planning dissertations and grant proposals.* Newbury Park, CA: Sage Publications, Inc.

London, M., & Smither, J. W. (2002). Feedback orientation, feedback culture, and the longitudinal performance management process. *Human Resource Management Review.* http://doi.org/10.1016/S1053-4822(01)00043-2

Lunenburg, F. C., & Irby, B. J. (2008). *Writing a Successful Thesis Or Dissertation: Tips and Strategies for Students in the Social and Behavioral Sciences.* Thousand Oaks, CA: Corwin Press. http://doi.org/10.1017/CBO9781107415324.004

Morissette, A. (1996). Ironic. ony/ATV Music Publishing LLC, Universal Music Publishing Group. Retrieved from http://www.prosseracademy.org/ourpages/auto/2006/10/15/116 0958883154/Ironic by Alanis Morissette.doc

Newton, I. (1959). *The Correspondence of Isaac Newton: 1661-1675, Vol 1.* (H. W. Turnbull, Ed.). London: Royal Society at the University Press.

O'Gorman, K., & MacIntosh, R. (2015). Mapping Research Methods. In K. O'Gorman & R. MacIntosh (Eds.), *Research Methods for Business & Management* (Second, pp. 50–74). Oxford: Goodfellow Publishers Limited.

Parkman, A. (2016). The Imposter Phenomenon in Higher Education : Incidence and Impact. *Journal of Higher Education Theory and Practice, 16*(1978), 51–61. Retrieved from http://search.proquest.com/openview/2aa0abe26e0eae30de19ed 5337a13b5f/1?pq-origsite=gscholar&cbl=766331

Publication Manual of the American Psychological Association. (2009) (Sixth). Washington, D.C.: American Psycological Association. Retrieved from http://auctions.canadaspace.com/detail_product/151842895050/publications/

Virginia, U. of. (n.d.). Problem statement Template. Retrieved from http://faculty.virginia.edu/schoolhouse/WP/probstattemplate.html

What Works Clearinghouse. (2014). *What Works Clearinghouse TM Procedures and Standards Handbook Version 3.0.* Washington, D.C. Retrieved from http://ies.ed.gov/ncee/wwc/pdf/reference_resources/wwc_procedures_v3_0_standards_handbook.pdf

Wiles, R., Crow, G., Heath, S., & Charles, V. (2008). The Management of Confidentiality and Anonymity in Social Research. *International Journal of Social Research Methodology*, *11*(5), 417–428. http://doi.org/10.1080/13645570701622231

Appendix A

Brainstorming Questions for Problem Statement Development
University of Virginia

(http://faculty.virginia.edu/schoolhouse/WP/probstattemplate.html)

Resolution

State your claim. Name something interesting that you've learned about the topic from reading/discussion/research.

Consequences

Why do you think the claim is interesting or important? What bigger questions has it helped you answer? What problems has it helped you to understand or solve?

Destabilizing Moment

What specific fact/concept/reading/etc. helped you to discover the claim?

Status Quo

Before you discovered the claim, what incorrect or incomplete opinion(s) did you hold about the topic?

Appendix B

Recommended References as You Begin Your Research

American Psychological Association. (2009, second printing). *Publication Manual of the American Psychological Association.* Washington, DC: Author.

Armstrong, R. L. (1974). Hypotheses: Why? When? How? *Phi Delta Kappan, 54,* 213-214.

Ary, D., Jacobs, L. C., & Sorensen, C. (2010). *Introduction to Research in Education.* Belmont, CA: Wadsworth.

Bryant, M. T. (2004). The portable dissertation advisor. Thousand Oaks, CA: Corwin Press.

Creswell, J. W. (2009). *Research design: Qualitative, quantitative, and mixed methods approaches.* Thousand Oaks, CA: Sage.

Eisner, E. W. (1998). *The enlightened Eye: Qualitative inquiry and the enhancement of educational practice.* Upper Saddle River, NJ: Merrill.

Field, A. (2009). *Discovering statistics using SPSS.* Thousand Oaks, CA: Sage.

Glatthorn, A. A. & Joyner, R. L. (2005). Writing the winning thesis or dissertation: A step-by-step guide. Thousand Oaks, CA: Corwin Press.

Heppner, P. P. & Heppner, M. J. (2004). Writing and publishing your thesis, dissertation and research: A guide for students in the helping professions. Belmont, CA: Cengage.

Krathwohl, D. R. (1988). *How to prepare a research proposal: Guidelines for funding and dissertations in the social and behavioral sciences.* Syracuse, NY: Syracuse University Press.

Lunenberg, F. C. & Irby, B. J. (2008). Writing a Successful thesis or dissertation: Tips and strategies for students in the social and behavioral sciences. Thousand Oaks, CA: Corwin Press.

Machi, L. A. & McEvoy, B. T. (2009). The Literature Review. Thousand Oaks, CA: Corwin Press.

Marshall, C., & Rossman, G. B. (1989). *Designing qualitative research*: Newbury Park, CA: Sage.

Paul, J. L. (2005). Introduction to the philosophies of research and criticism in education and the social sciences. Upper Saddle River, NJ: Pearson.

Roberts, C. M. (2010). The dissertation journey: A practical and comprehensive guide to planning, writing, and defending your dissertation. Thousand Oaks, CA: Corwin Press.

Sutter, W. N. (2006). Introduction to educational research: A critical thinking approach. Thousand Oaks, CA: Sage.

Thomas, R. M. & Brubaker, D. L. (2008). Theses and dissertations: A guide to planning, research and writing. Thousand Oaks, CA: Corwin Press.

Warner, R. M. (2008). *Applied statistics: From bivariate through multivariate techniques*. Thousand Oaks, CA: Sage.

Wiersma, W. (1995). *Research methods in education: An introduction* (Sixth edition). Boston: Allyn and Bacon.

61758398R00109

Made in the USA
Lexington, KY
19 March 2017